D0855512

Third World
Multinationals

Third World Multinationals
The Rise of Foreign
Investment from
Developing Countries

Louis T. Wells, Jr.

The MIT Press
Cambridge, Massachusetts
London, England

This material is based upon work supported by the National Science Foundation under Grant No. PRA78-10238. Any opinions, findings, conclusions, or recommendations expressed in this publication are those of the author and do not necessarily reflect the views of the Foundation.

This book was set in Palatino
by The MIT Press Computergraphics Department
and printed and bound by The Murray Printing Co.
in the United States of America.

Library of Congress Calaloging in Publication Data

Wells, Louis T.
  Third World multinationals.

  Bibliography: p.
  Includes index.
  1. Underdeveloped areas—International business enterprises. 2. Underdeveloped areas—Corporations.
  I. Title.
  HD2755.5.W44 1983   338.8′881724   82–21662
  ISBN 0-262-23113-1

Contents

Contents

Acknowledgments

A book that reports on a subject as broad as the topic of this study, covering Latin America, Asia, and Africa, can hardly be the work of one person. This book draws freely from the ideas and data of researchers who were working closely with me and from other writers.

My interest in Third World multinationals grew out of a study on choice of technology that I conducted in Indonesia for Professor Mohammed Sadli, then minister of manpower. That study, sponsored by the Harvard Institute for International Development, brought me inside several subsidiaries of firms from other developing countries. The differences between those subsidiaries and the subsidiaries of multinationals from other countries were striking and had not been systematically studied.

Some of the hypotheses for this research on Third World multinationals had their beginnings with K. Balakrishnan, who proposed to write a doctoral dissertation on Indian joint ventures abroad, a work that was never completed. The Thai data and much of the accompanying analysis that appear in this book come from Donald Lecraw, who wrote a dissertation at Harvard on choice of technology in Thailand. Lecraw followed his Thai study with other research in Southeast Asia, on which I have also drawn. For Mauritius and the Philippines, I have reported data from the doctoral thesis prepared by Vinod Busjeet on multinationals from developing countries. Both Lecraw's and Busjeet's data have been invaluable to me.

Carlos Cordeiro conducted interviews in India for the study and produced an undergraduate thesis at Harvard on the foreign investments of Indian firms. Sonia Dula collected data from firms in Mexico. Sergio Koreisha accompanied me for interviews in Argentina, Brazil, and Peru. He provided ideas as well as Portuguese and Spanish vocabulary.

Early in my research I met members of the Instituto para la Integración de America Latina (INTAL), in Buenos Aires, who were examining Latin American joint ventures. This resulted in a fruitful exchange of ideas, data, and some interview notes. In 1979, the East-West Center in Honolulu organized a conference, "Third World Multinationals," under the direction of Krishna Kumar. I have used ideas and data from the participants in that conference.

The conceptual underpinnings of the study derive largely from the works of Stephen Hymer, Raymond Vernon, Oliver Williamson, John Dunning, Peter Buckley, and Mark Casson. Raymond Vernon, Max Hall, Donald Lessard, Donald Lecraw, and anonymous reviewers provided valuable comments on drafts of various chapters.

The work of recording data from my notes, others' notes, and from published sources fell primarily on Nathan Fagre, Mark Worrell, Carlos Cordeiro, Sonia Dula, and Liliana Scagliotti. It was Kristin Manos whose hard work and concern finally got a computerized data bank into operation. Most of the calculations and tabulations from the data were performed by Sushil Vachani. The translation of my handwriting into properly spelled, typed words was done by Madelyn Kissock.

Of course such a study could not have succeeded without the cooperation of a large number of government officials and company managers in developing countries. Many prefer not to be named, and the list of those who helped would in any case be too long to provide here. One company, however, must be singled out for its special hospitality, even outdistancing the high norms set by a number of other firms. Packages Limited, of Lahore, hosted me and my family for two weeks in Pakistan. Through its managing director, Babar Ali, I came to know one Third World multinational in considerable depth. I should note that only one firm refused an interview and that the vast majority were very cooperative in providing information.

Funds for this study came primarily from the National Science Foundation under Grant No. PRA78-10238. NSF funds were supplemented by start-up money from the Division of Research of the Harvard Business School. Expenses for work in India came from the Ford Foundation (for the uncompleted work of K. Balakrishnan) and Harvard's Center for International Affairs (for C. Cordeiro).

Third World
Multinationals

1   The New Multinationals

In 1928, the Argentine manufacturer S.I.A.M. di Tella established a subsidiary in Brazil to produce gasoline pumps. At about the same time, the company set up manufacturing projects in Chile and Uruguay and commercial offices in New York and London. This book is about that firm and many other firms in developing nations that have recently made direct investments abroad.

The reader who has been exposed to the vast literature on multinational enterprises based in the United States, Europe, and Japan and who has been impressed with the figures showing the importance of those firms is entitled to ask whether investors from the developing countries are significant enough for him to read a book on the subject. It is true that when Raymond Vernon's *Sovereignty at Bay* appeared in 1971 firms based in the developing countries had invested only a small fraction of the $70 billion that U.S.-based multinationals had invested overseas.[1] Twenty years ago, only a few pioneering firms from the developing countries had established foreign footholds. Several Argentine firms had begun manufacturing operations in nearby countries before the Second World War, and, to be sure, quite a number of banks from the developing countries had already set up overseas offices. There were only a few other examples.

In the 1950s and 1960s, it would have been difficult to imagine that developing countries could offer the environment that would generate many local manufacturing firms with competitive advantages sufficient for international competition. Change, however, has been rapid. In 1959, it is reported, Singapore had only two factories: a brewery, which accounted for 75 percent of the island's manufacturing output, and a rubber shoe factory.[2] From 1960 to 1970, manufacturing output grew at an average annual rate of 13 percent; through the 1970s, it grew at more than 9 percent. By 1976, Singapore's firms were adding some

$700 million of value per year in manufacturing and had invested at least $130 million abroad.

The manufacturing sectors of other developing countries have also grown rapidly. Manufacturing output in a number of countries had, by 1976, reached the scale of industry in some of the smaller industrialized countries. India's manufacturing sector, for example, was almost as large as Sweden's. Brazil's was approaching that of Canada; Mexico's had exceeded those of The Netherlands and Belgium.[3]

For these and a number of other developing countries, the old stereotypes are dramatically out of data. No longer are they simply agricultural economies or exporters of raw materials for the advanced countries. Moreover, manufacturing activity does not consist solely of sweatshops that rely on low-wage and low-skilled workers. Rather, factories in growing developing countries produce steel, paper, and plastics as well as textiles, household appliances, and pots and pans. There is evidence, albeit sketchy, to suggest that the industrial firms in those developing countries are undertaking substantial research and development activities.[4]

The smaller industrialized countries have produced their share of multinational enterprises: Philips from The Netherlands, Atlas Copco from Sweden, Massey Ferguson from Canada, to name a few. It should not, then, be surprising that the NICs (newly industrializing countries) of the developing world have generated a new wave of multinationals. The first Indian manufacturing investment abroad went into production in 1960; foreign investments by Hong Kong firms began about the same time. But by the late 1970s Indian and Hong Kong firms alone held at least 370 overseas manufacturing subsidiaries.

It is very difficult to put together accurate figures on the size of direct investment emanating from the developing countries. However, the stock of direct investments held abroad from the developing countries was at least $5–10 billion by 1980, as best one can estimate from official sources and from some careful guesses (see appendix for sources of data). To supplement official sources, my associates and I have assembled a "data bank" containing facts on 1,964 overseas subsidiaries and branches established by firms based in developing countries. The parent firms numbered 963. The subsidiaries and branches were located in 125 host countries, and 938 of them were engaged in manufacturing. The numbers are significant, and the fact that so many investments have appeared in such a short time suggests that the overall numbers are likely to be considerably more impressive in the next few years.

Already investors from other developing countries are extremely important to certain host countries. In Indonesia, since 1967, if petroleum and mining are excluded, other developing countries have accounted for some 31 percent of all foreign investment projects and 21 percent of their value.[5] This is more than Japanese or North American or European investments. In Thailand and Singapore, a third or more of all foreign investment appears to come from other developing countries. For governments in host countries, decisions on the costs and benefits of foreign investors from other developing countries already have a significant impact on development.

Moreover, a large proportion of the parent firms are concentrated in several developing countries. The investments have originated primarily in countries of South and Southeast Asia and Latin America, in large part from the newly industrializing countries. It is a rare foreign direct investor whose home is in the Middle East; a still rarer one, in Africa.[6] For the home countries, the emergence of firms that want to go abroad poses political and economic questions. What is the impact on development at home? What is the impact of policies toward locally owned firms on the ability of the country to act in its own interests toward multinationals from elsewhere? Which local enterprises, if any, should be restricted from going abroad? Which should be encouraged?[7]

Whatever the overall figures or the figures for particular countries, they do not fully capture the importance of foreign investors from developing countries. In many ways, they are quite different from the more traditional multinationals from the United States, Europe, and Japan. Some of the differences lead to hopes that such investors can make a special kind of contribution to the development of poor countries. The technology that they transfer and the products that they make, this study will argue, are generated from the conditions of the home countries and thus might be especially well suited to the needs of other developing countries. In the jargon of the development literature, some of these firms offer "appropriate technology" and "appropriate products." There is some evidence, too, that these investors offer their products at a low price to the consumer and, perhaps, their know-how at a low cost to the host country.

Further, the firms appear to conform to some of the demands of their developing country hosts. They are particularly likely to share ownership with local investors. Some 90 percent of the manufacturing subsidiaries of developing country parents identified in this study are joint ventures, compared with 40 percent for U.S.-owned multinationals. Moreover, the Third World firms seem to grant a great deal of autonomy to their subsidiary managers.

Subsidiaries of developing country parent companies are almost all in other developing countries, in contrast to those of multinationals from the United States, which have historically established their foreign manufacturing plants first and most frequently in other advanced countries. In fact, the majority of investments of firms based in developing countries are to countries with a lower level of development than the home countries. More than 65 percent of the subsidiaries identified in this study were in countries with less value added in manufacturing than that of the parent countries (see table 1.1). The majority of investments to countries with greater value added were from Singapore, which is very industrialized but has only a small total value added in manufacturing. If per capita GNP is taken as the measure, the results are similar, but Singapore is no longer an exception. The few cases of investments in countries that are richer than the home country, according to per capita GNP, are mostly from India, where this measure understates the size of the industrial sector.

The transfer of technology from developing country to developing country, and especially to the poorer countries, makes the parent firm from a developing country a concrete example of South-South cooperation; it is one of the few. With "collective self-reliance" a part of the rhetoric of the North-South dialogue, these investors have entered the picture. They offer hope of less dependence on firms from the rich countries of the North for the technology needed for development. The United Nations Conference on Trade and Development (UNCTAD) commissioned what may have been the first papers on "developing country joint ventures," as they are usually labeled by the international organizations.[8] Recently the U.N. Industrial Development Organization (UNIDO), the U.N. Centre on Transnational Corporations (UNCTC), the Food and Agricultural Organization (FAO), and the International Labour Office (ILO) joined UNCTAD.[9] UNIDO has continued to sponsor work on the subject.[10] Most of the U.N. organizations emphasize the role of "developing country joint ventures" in self-reliance in the South and on their contribution to the New International Economic Order.[11]

Another characteristic of foreign investors from developing countries makes them of special interest to a somewhat different group of international organizations. Most of the investment of these firms is in neighboring countries. For instance, of 494 foreign manufacturing subsidiaries of a parent firm in Southeast Asia, 428 were in the same region;

Table 1.1
Number of subsidiaries of parent firms from developing countries (1975)

Manufacturing value added of parent's country ($ millions)	Manufacturing value added of subsidiary's country ($ millions)							
	Less than 500	500–849	850–854	855–899	900–999	1,000–1,499	1,500–1,999	2,000 or more
Less than 500	23	15	47	0	6	23	2	5
500–849	1	1	37	1	0	2	0	3
850–854	1	0	0	0	0	2	0	0
855–899	30	26	99	0	0	20	15	7
900–999	18	0	0	0	0	0	0	2
1,000–1,499	18	2	25	1	0	2	3	3
1,500–1,999	27	15	34	3	3	52	11	18
2,000 or more	76	73	23	1	14	20	19	51

118 of 157 subsidiaries of a parent firm in Latin America were in the same region. Because of the regional investment patterns, organizations interested in regional economic integration have seen local multinationals as vehicles for reaching their goals. The Instituto para la Integración de America Latina (INTAL), in particular, has promoted such firms in Latin America and conducted research on locally based multinationals and on barriers to their spread within the region.[12]

This study argues that some of the characteristics of Third World multinationals are beneficial to the development of both host and home countries but that new multinationals carry with them some important costs, including limited access to export markets, technology that may be considered out of date, and extensive use of expatriate personnel. Moreover, most of the Third World multinationals are quite different from the joint ventures envisioned by some of the international organizations. Rather than being equal partnerships in a new enterprise, most are parent-subsidiary relationships that are not so different from ventures set up by traditional multinationals from the industrialized countries. Whatever the characteristics of the firms, their future does not seem as unclouded as some of their supporters might claim.

The new multinationals will affect not only the developing countries but in some cases will compete with traditional multinationals from the advanced countries. They already challenge markets held by the established firms and, by providing alternatives to host countries, weaken the bargaining power of certain traditional multinationals in their negotiations with developing countries. On the other hand, the new multinationals have, on occasion, combined with multinationals from the advanced countries in mutually beneficial joint activities.

The apparent differences between the foreign investors from developing countries and the multinationals from the industrialized countries pose a major challenge to theories that purport to explain foreign direct investment. Can the same concepts that have proved useful in studies of the traditional multinationals help in understanding the new foreign investors? My contention is that they can and that the process of applying the concepts to the new firms aids in understanding both the concepts and the different kinds of multinationals.

Terminology

This book is about foreign direct investment from developing countries. Consequently, it covers enterprises with parent firms in developing countries only if those parents establish branches or subsidiaries in other countries. For an enterprise to be included in the study, its overseas operations must have some kind of ownership tie to the originating firm in the home country.[13] To be a direct investment, the subsidiary or branch must, to some extent, be under the control of the parent firm. In most cases, such investments are undertaken by a parent firm that goes abroad with management and know-how to do something similar to what it was doing at home. Foreign direct investment does not include portfolio investments or other purely financial flows, even though these are important, particularly for the oil-rich countries.[14] Further, the book does not concern itself with the emigrant entrepreneur who decides to try his fortune abroad. Indian, Lebanese, Syrian, and overseas Chinese businessmen have for decades migrated to a number of developing countries and carried with them their skills and, sometimes, capital. They provide an interesting topic for research. In fact, their activities will play some role in this study, but only because they have had, on many occasions, an influence on the direct investors that are the subject of the research at hand.

To be considered in this study as a parent firm in a developing country, an enterprise must be owned by nationals of that country. Thus, Volkswagen of Brazil, which holds equity in Volkswagen of Peru, is not included in this study, since its ultimate ownership is German. Nevertheless, some such ventures are similar to the firms reported on in this study. Sometimes the subsidiaries of the traditional multinationals have adapted product or production techniques to developing country markets. Those subsidiaries are called on later to transfer knowledge to other developing countries. The resulting behavior may be different from that typical of the ultimate parent enterprise. Like Volkswagen of Brazil, because the ultimate ownership usually is in the advanced countries, firms registered as coming from the usual tax havens (Panama, the Bahamas, New Hebrides [Vanuatu], Liberia, and The Netherlands Antilles) are not included in this study unless there was some clear evidence to link them back to a parent in a developing country. An attempt has been made to eliminate advanced country firms that have used Hong Kong simply as a point of registry.

Not only must the ownership be in the hands of developing country nationals but management must be from the local culture. Thus, the British-managed firms of Hong Kong, such as Jardine-Matheson and the Swire Group, were not included.[15] The British in Hong Kong seem to be first and foremost British. On the other hand, when managers appear to have been integrated into the local business culture, their firms have been included regardless of the managers' ethnic origin. Accordingly, Argentine firms managed by Anglo-Argentinians have been included. Although Anglo-Argentinians retain, in many cases, English language schools and English clubs, their businesses seem to be run much like firms whose owners or managers are Argentinians of Spanish or Italian descent.

Similarly, since their foreign investment decisions were not usually made by local management or when the firm was locally owned, we did not include firms for which ownership and headquarters have very recently shifted from an industrialized country to a developing one.[16] Thus, Sime Darby, once a British firm but now a Malaysian one, is not included.[17] Its overseas subsidiaries were simply acquired by the Malaysians as a result of the acquisition of the parent enterprise. But such firms presumably do eventually behave like other local firms, as management is increasingly made up of nationals. Thus, Bunge y Born, with more than three-quarters of a century as an Argentine firm, was included in this study.[18] Admittedly, the line is on occasion a fine one for each of these exclusions. For example, we have included Textile Alliance, Ltd., a Hong Kong firm owned largely by a Japanese firm (45 percent) and Jardine-Matheson. The Japanese interest was acquired only recently; and management seems to be in the hands of Chinese. Luckily, such difficult judgments had to be made for only a few enterprises.

To avoid confusion, the term "developing country" should also be defined. In this study, the developing countries are those so classified by the United Nations Centre on Transnational Corporations. They are the countries with market economies in Latin America, Africa (except South Africa), Oceania (except New Zealand and Australia), and Asia (except Japan). Thus, the study does not cover investments from low-income European countries, such as Portugal, Spain, and Greece; Israel; or the centrally planned economies of the Soviet Union, the Communist countries of Eastern Europe, and the People's Republic of China.[19] It should be understood, however, that some of the most active investors in the developing countries covered here are ethnic Chinese—in Hong Kong, Taiwan, and Singapore.

The term "Third World" will appear only occasionally here. It is not a very satisfying term because it means different things to different people. Whenever I use it, I simply mean developing countries.

The firms from developing countries that are making foreign direct investments can be called "the new multinationals" if one broadly defines "multinational enterprise" to mean an enterprise that owns facilities in more than one country. The story is different if a stricter definition is used. For example, in Harvard Business School's recent Multinational Enterprise Project, a U.S.-based firm was not counted as a multinational enterprise unless it had manufacturing subsidiaries in six or more foreign countries. By that standard, only 6 of our 963 developing country parent firms would qualify—two from India, two from Hong Kong, one from Colombia, and one from Mexico.[20]

Data and Methodology

Data on the foreign investments of firms from developing countries are hard to come by. Some governments in developing countries provide information on investment outflows, but the figures are, in many cases, quite incomplete. A number of governments provide some information on inflows from developing countries, but these numbers are also frequently unreliable and rarely match the reported outflows from the investors' home countries.[21]

In an effort to learn more about individual investments in a wide range of countries, my associates and I surveyed a wide range of publications (such as *The Economist*, the *Far Eastern Economic Review*, and *Boletín Sobre Inversiones y Empresas Latinoamericanas*) and national directories (such as *Guia Intervest*, Rio de Janeiro, 1978). We also obtained access to additional, unpublished material from governments in Indonesia, India, Thailand, the Philippines, and Mauritius.

Particularly important to our efforts to collect statistics and learn more about the decisions being made by managers were interviews that we conducted in parent firms and subsidiaries in Taiwan, Hong Kong, the Philippines, Indonesia, India, Sri Lanka, Mauritius, Mexico, Peru, Brazil, and Argentina. In total, managers in some 150 enterprises were interviewed.

The data bank that was constructed from government sources, publications, and interviews could hardly be said to contain a random sample of foreign investors from developing countries. On the other hand, there is little reason to believe that the biases of the data bank would be the same as those of official published sources; yet, the two bodies of data accord strikingly well insofar as they can be compared. This is shown in table 1.2. Official sources reported on the total dollar

Table 1.2
Investment abroad and number of foreign subsidiaries of fifteen developing country firms

Home country of parent firms	Home government sources	Data bank	
	Foreign direct investment ($ million)[a]	Number of subsidiaries of all kinds	Number of manufacturing subsidiaries
Hong Kong	976[b]	325	202
India	88[c]	215	168
Argentina	38[d]	146	76
Singapore	370[e]	89	57
Philippines	276[f]	66	26
Brazil	41[e]	147	25
Korea	71[g]	155	25
Mexico	23	62	22
Peru	4[e]	37	18
Colombia	35[e]	37	18
Venezuela	64[e]	18	9
Chile	14[e]	11	7
Bolivia	3[e]	0	0
Ecuador	19[e]	2	0
Paraguay	0[e]	2	0

a. Data were not collected in the same year for all countries but between 1975 and 1978. Some figures represent only investments in countries in the same region. It is not always clear whether figures are for equity or for total investment.
b. Includes only Thailand, Indonesia, the Philippines, and Taiwan. Calculated from U.N. Centre on Transnational Corporations, *Transnational Corporations in World Development* (New York: United Nations, 1978), pp. 246–247, and data from the Taiwan Investment Commission.
c. Data from "A New Dimension for India," *Far Eastern Economic Review*, May 30, 1980, p. 68. The actual investment figures are probably much higher than the $88 million reported to the Indian government.
d. Data from Eduardo White, "The International Projection of Firms from Latin American Countries," in Krishna Kumar and Maxwell McLeod, eds., *Multinationals from Developing Countries* (Lexington, Mass.: Lexington Books, 1981).
e. Includes only Indonesia and Malaysia. Data from *Far Eastern Economic Review*, October 19, 1979, p. 81, and the Indonesian Board of Investments.
f. Data from Yung W. Rhee and Larry E. Westphal, "A Note on Exports of Technology from the Republics of China and Korea," mimeograph (1979), p. 22. Rhee and Westphal's data came from *The Naeway Business Journal*, June 18, 1978.
g. Only $14 million for manufacturing.

amounts of outgoing investments from sixteen countries, but I have excluded Taiwan from the table because its official figures on outgoing investments were in extreme disagreement with data from other countries on incoming Taiwan investments. The ranking of the countries by total dollar investment from official sources and the ranking by total number of subsidiaries identified for the data bank were very close (Spearman's rank correlation coefficient is 0.82). The rankings were even closer when only manufacturing subsidiaries were taken into account (0.90).[22]

Not surprisingly, the countries with "too many" subsidiaries in the data bank (a ranking two or more places above that shown by official data) were countries in which information had been collected through interviews. The information in the data bank was more complete for those countries than for places researched only in publications.

The coverage of regions is not even. I and my associates did more work in Asia than in Latin America. Nevertheless, the results of research done by INTAL[23] are reported in this study. Those findings and the interviews we did conduct in Mexico, Brazil, Argentina, and Peru suggest that the factors influencing Latin American firms are similar to those that influence Asian firms.

The reader will also note that certain hypotheses were tested using data from only a small number of countries. This problem reflects the difficulty of obtaining necessary information. Indonesia appears frequently in the analysis as a result of my own work in that country, Thailand as a result of Donald Lecraw's research, and Mauritius and the Philippines as a result of the work undertaken by Vinod Busjeet. Indonesia and Thailand do not seem atypical of countries with considerable foreign investment serving the local market. When comparisons could be made between patterns observed in Indonesia and Thailand and patterns in other countries, the results were similar. On the other hand, a large percentage of the investors in the Philippines and, particularly, in Mauritius, were of a special kind. Firms had located there to export to third countries. Data about such investors are typical of only a small subset of firms in this study. As a result, they are used cautiously in the research.

A better understanding of foreign investors from the developing countries requires, in many cases, that they be compared to foreign investors from the industrialized countries and, occasionally, to firms purely local to the host countries. For the comparisons with firms from the industrialized countries, two kinds of information were used. First, the data banks created for Harvard Business School's Multinational Enterprise Project provided coverage of large multinationals from the United States, Europe, and Japan. Second, some governments made available information on subsidiaries in their countries owned by investors of various nationalities. For comparisons with purely local firms, information was extremely limited and came primarily from government sources in Thailand and interviews in other countries. In this kind of comparison and in a few other cases, the scarce evidence means that support for certain propositions is not very convincing. The evidence is presented nevertheless, since it is the best available.

The comparisons between multinationals from the advanced countries and the new ones from the developing countries play an important role in measuring the kinds and relative sizes of net benefits that the different types of investors can bring to bear on the development process. To understand those differences, one must understand why multinationals exist and what determines their characteristics.

2   Understanding Foreign Direct Investment

There is no single theory of foreign investment to which one can turn in the search for an understanding of investors from developing countries. In economics, as in the physical sciences, the elegant, systematic theories carry the analyst only a certain distance. When the phenomenon must be understood at the micro level, the elegant theories must give way to concepts that are partial and less rigorous.

The elegant theories of economics derive from assumptions of perfect competition. In the world of neoclassical economics, direct foreign investment has little place.[1] With no external economies and no barriers to trade, and with costless information, international trade is the only form of international involvement, since trade will equalize factor prices.[2] If trade is not frictionless, capital might move internationally, but it should move from the well-endowed countries to the poorly-endowed ones—from the industrialized countries to the developing ones. When risk is introduced into traditional theory, more complex investment flows are predicted,[3] but neither trade barriers nor risk offer adequate explanations of the ownership and control associated with foreign direct investment.

Although work based largely on neoclassical models has been successful in explaining certain aspects of foreign investment flows from the advanced countries,[4] the theories have done little to answer the kinds of questions that must be addressed in this book to determine why firms from developing countries invest abroad, how they compare with foreign investors from other countries, what their overseas activities mean for other companies and for governments, and what their future might be.

The need for diversification explains some of the actions of foreign investors from developing countries, but most of this study relies on three sets of concepts that are quite different from neoclassical theory.

They have proved particularly useful in understanding multinationals from the United States, Europe, and Japan. The concepts are based on the assumptions that certain firms have skills and information that are not easily available to others; that managers are risk-averse, face costs in acquiring information about alternatives, and as a result are likely to select alternatives that satisfy their goals rather than maximize profits; and that certain kinds of transactions can be more effectively conducted within the same firm than between two unrelated firms. Further, barriers to trade play an important role in explaining direct investment.

Firm-Specific Advantages

Unlike neoclassical theory, recently developed explanations of foreign investment rest partly on the argument that most firms must have some advantages over other firms before they can operate successfully abroad.[5] The need for advantages is a product of the nature of nationalistic governments and the high cost of information. When a firm from one country operates in another country, it incurs a set of costs that are not faced by local firms. It has an extra burden of overhead that results from the need to communicate between the subsidiary and the home office. As a consequence, it must support managers and technicians who are more costly than those a local firm hires. In addition, it suffers from a lack of familiarity with the local environment and thus is likely to make marketing mistakes, misjudge local norms for compensation of labor, and so on. Moreover, policies of many host governments discriminate against the foreign investor in subtle or overt ways. To offset such disadvantages, a successful foreign firm must usually have an asset or skill that is not possessed by a local firm.

Research has emphasized that the special conditions of the home market seem to play an important role in generating the advantages that multinational enterprises from industrialized countries exploit.[6] The evidence is now quite convincing that the familiarity of managers with their home markets and the lack of intimate information about other markets leads them to concentrate their innovative activities on satisfying nearby needs.[7]

American managers have been especially likely to seize on products, processes, or marketing techniques that appeal to a high-income market or save on skilled labor. Compared to other countries, the United States long offered a uniquely large market for high-income products. Consequently, it was U.S. entrepreneurs who innovated mass produced automobiles, television sets, and instant cameras. Moreover, compared to other countries, skilled labor in the United States was for a long time scarce and expensive. Thus, it was American entrepreneurs who responded to this scarcity with sewing machines, computers, and so on.

Once introduced in the U.S. markets, such products and processes typically found growing markets abroad, as increasing incomes and labor costs made foreign markets similar to the home market previously faced by American firms. Thus, the innovating firms had an opportunity to profit from their advantages in foreign markets.[8]

Like their U.S. counterparts, European firms have responded to their special environments with suitable innovations.[9] Although each country has had its own peculiar pattern, the continental countries overall have historically been more likely than U.S. firms to innovate processes or adapt products to save raw materials. European firms also have designed many products to appeal to customers with lower incomes than those typical of the United States.[10] Thus, most European cars are smaller and more economical to operate than American ones, and European home appliances are made simpler and for smaller living areas than American appliances. Although the adaptations were undertaken to enable European firms to compete in their home countries, their products and processes challenged American firms in poorer countries and in certain market segments of the United States. The Japanese have provided a similar story.[11]

Moving from American to European to Japanese firms, one can imagine a ladder of technologies that have given various multinationals their initial advantages abroad. Through the 1960s, American firms were strong in high-income, labor-saving products; European and Japanese firms were strong in somewhat lower income products and in products and processes that saved raw materials and capital.

Firms do not hold on to their advantages forever. Companies abroad copy and sometimes improve on what the innovators did. When American automobile manufacturers went to Europe, their mass production know-how was far ahead of that of their European competitors. At the time, the Americans began by manufacturing cars very much like those they made at home. After the Americans demonstrated the opportunities, the Europeans and later the Japanese mastered the techniques required for mass-producing automobiles and manufactured products more suitable to local demand. In the face of such competition, some firms are able to develop new competitive advantages; others face a decline in their international position.

Until recently, it was quite easy to describe differences among the markets of Japan, European countries, and the United States, but those differences in home markets that led to different innovations have gradually diminished. As a result, in the 1980s it is increasingly difficult to predict the national source of a wide range of innovations.[12] As income levels and wage rates have converged, labor-saving or high-income products or processes now seem about as likely to come from European or Japanese firms as from American firms. Similarly, U.S. firms now face incentives to save on raw materials and capital much like those that have for some time confronted European or Japanese enterprises.

The markets of the developing countries, however, remain quite apart from those of the industrialized nations. The differences seem to lead to identifiable types of innovations by firms in the developing countries.[13] The argument in this study is that when they go to other developing countries, the innovative firms have found that their differences give them an edge over potential local competitors and over multinationals from the advanced countries.

It should be noted, however, that some firms from the developing countries have not based their foreign investments on an innovative edge, and not all the multinationals from America, Europe, or Japan have been built on such an advantage. Some of these exceptions will appear in this book, but the dominant theme is that special kinds of innovations have given certain firms from developing countries opportunities to profit from foreign markets.

Motivations for Investment

Not every firm that develops advantages over its competitors exploits them abroad. Indeed, the fact that some firms with advantages never do should not be surprising in light of recent studies that show that managers have limited information at their disposal, that additional information comes at a cost, and that managers are risk-averse and tend to be content with "satisfactory returns." To use the firm's advantages abroad, the manager must acquire information about foreign markets at additional cost. If opportunities at home are adequate, the manager may simply never incur those costs.

If the firm does exploit its advantages in foreign markets, it is likely to prefer exports over other approaches. In this way, it can profit from its return on technology, marketing skills, or other advantages and avoid the need to collect as much information and risk as much money as would be required for foreign investment.

Even though exports might be the preferred way of exploiting advantages abroad, the firm often finds that the opportunities are eventually restricted. Transportation costs and tariffs may, up to a point, simply be passed on to the foreign consumer, but when imitators begin to appear abroad, the firm's ability to pass on such costs is limited. Moreover, as importing countries see the opportunity for local manufacture of the products, they may raise the barriers to imports.

Investment in a plant or other facility located inside the market is one possible response to such restrictions and is particularly likely to be undertaken by the firm that initially exported to the market.[14] If a manager from such a firm has already acquired considerable information about the market by selling in it, he will perceive fewer risks than the manager of a firm without that experience. Further, the experienced manager usually has developed a vested interest in the market. With his performance evaluation based partly on returns from that market, he is likely to become a "champion" within the firm to support investment when that step is essential to defend the company's market share. The existence of such a champion is in many cases an important element in a firm's decision to undertake foreign investment in the face of perceived risk and uncertainty.

The pattern just described is typical of the firms in this study. Nevertheless, there are a number of important exceptions, such as firms that responded to restrictions on their exports by establishing manufacturing subsidiaries in a third country.

Defense of export markets is not the only motivation for going abroad, but the majority of foreign subsidiaries set up by developing countries were undertaken for defensive reasons, and only when threatened.

Investment or License?

The firm with an advantage and the motivation to use that advantage abroad has alternatives to investment. It might, for example, sell its skills to a foreign enterprise. The usual mechanism is a simple licensing agreement. Other vehicles are turnkey plants and management contracts.

Whatever the method, the fee paid by the recipient of the advantages can be set to capture the lion's share of the rent on the special knowledge.

In many cases, companies do turn to the "market" and sell to foreign firms know-how, trade names, and other assets that give them competitive advantages. But the firms in this study have not exploited their competitive advantages abroad through such market arrangements. In some cases, they have concluded that contracts pose problems of security that are not easily overcome. In other cases, negotiations for such arrangements are too difficult because of the imbalance of information available to the parties or the number of contingencies that must be covered.

Thus there are circumstances in which a firm is better off if it establishes its own branches, joint ventures, or wholly owned subsidiaries overseas. Identifying those circumstances has proved to be a valuable contribution to knowledge of foreign investors[15] and is an important part of this study.

3

Small-Scale
Manufacturing as a
Competitive Advantage

Since much of the research on multinationals from the advanced countries has emphasized their technological advantages, it should not be surprising to discover that technical know-how also provides many foreign investors from the developing countries with competitive advantages that enable them to survive abroad. The latter's technological advantages are of a very special kind; they reflect the investors' home markets and give the firms considerable potential for contributing to the development process in the poorer countries.

Small-Scale Markets

One particular feature in developing countries that gives firms in this study an edge abroad is the small size of the markets for most manufactured goods. Entrepreneurs in developing countries have a special propensity to respond to that characteristic.

If firms in the developing countries simply import manufacturing technology commonly used in the industrialized countries, the factories are likely to be too large for their market. In 1959, for instance, Sri Lanka turned to the Soviet Union for help in establishing iron and steel works. The first plant was to be a rolling mill. The smallest rolling mill the Russians had built had a capacity of 60,000 tons of steel per year. (Even this plant was very small by the standards of industrialized countries; the average steel mill elsewhere produced some one million tons per year.) But total Sri Lankan demand was only 35,000 tons. Moreover, this demand was for a wider variety of products than the Russian mill could supply and the export potential was poor. In spite of the scale problem, the Sri Lankans, like many other developing countries, acquired the large-scale technology instead of turning to, say, India for small, manually operated rolling mills.[1] As a result, Sri

Lanka utilized only about a quarter of its installed capacity for rolled steel products in 1973 and continued to import rolled steel products, largely of kinds not produced by the existing plant.

Faced with small markets for many products, entrepreneurs in developing countries can increase profits if they can adapt technology to small-scale manufacture. In most cases, they start with technology from an industrialized country and adapt it later. Of 52 Indian parent firms interviewed, 42 reported that they obtained their original technology abroad, but 47 also reported that over half of their technology was "indigenous" by the time of the interview (table 3.1). One Indian firm that processes edible oil illustrates the pattern. It began operations in India in 1917 with copra crushing equipment imported from the United States. By 1976, it was using entirely Indian equipment. The local equipment was not slavishly copied from the earlier imported machinery; it was changed in response to Indian conditions. In many cases, locally adapted technology was eventually exported to foreign subsidiaries, as is apparent from the fact that "Indian machinery" was the source of know-how in most of the foreign investments for which data were available.

A manufacturing process might be scaled down in various ways. When larger plants consist primarily of duplicate pieces of equipment, such as spinning and weaving plants, little innovation is required. Some of the small-scale plants observed in this study simply used fewer pieces of equipment than large-scale plants. In other cases, adaptation to small scale means the substitution of batch processing for mass production. Packages Limited of Pakistan manufactures paper containers in short runs, and a Philippine firm manufactures pharmaceutical products in batches. Sometimes assembly lines are dropped and semifinished products are moved in batches from work station to work station, such as in several flashlight battery manufacturers in Indonesia. On occasion, labor may be substituted directly for machines. Thus, steel auto bodies may be fashioned by hand to avoid the high fixed cost of dies. To facilitate manual work, some products are redesigned. Jeepney bodies in the Philippines, for example, were designed with simple bends instead of the curves typical of auto bodies in richer countries. Similarly, a Hong Kong firm redesigned appliances to use fewer molded plastic parts. The adaptation of the manufacturing process to small scale may sometimes involve a completely different technology, such as the use of fiberglass instead of steel for auto bodies. In some cases, factories for small-scale manufacture use machinery that has been especially

Table 3.1
Sources of technology of Indian parent firms and their foreign manufacturing subsidiaries (1977)

Sector	Source of parents' original technology			Source of foreign subsidiaries' technology			Source of parents' 1977 technology	
	India	Foreign collaboration	Imports of foreign machinery	India	Japan	Other foreign countries	At least 50 percent indigenous	Mostly imported
Paper and cardboard	1	2	2	7			5	
Chemicals, soaps, and drugs	2	1	3	8		1	4	2
Edible oils	1	2	1	9			4	
Automobile ancillary	1	5	3	7	1	1	8	1
Foods, beverages, and confectionery	1	3	1	5		3	3	2
Construction			3	3			3	
Miscellaneous light ancillary	1	5	3	12		1	9	
Heavy industry			3	4			3	
Textiles	3	2	3	4	1	3	8	
Total	10	20	22	59	2	9	47	5

Source: Interviews conducted by Carlos Cordeiro.

designed for lower output levels. A carpet maker in the Philippines uses 16-inch looms; many U.S. firms use 200-inch looms. Some factories rely on multipurpose machines to manufacture at small volumes. Thus, parts for various products may be made on standard lathes or bent with simple equipment. One firm planning for a capacity of 20,000 refrigerators per year chose multipurpose equipment for the production of cabinets. The machines could be adjusted for various models of refrigerators and for other appliances. Sometimes workers may be used, much like multipurpose machines, for a number of tasks in the production process.[2]

It is exactly these kinds of small-scale technology that were exported by many of the firms in this study. Information from Lecraw's work in Thailand bears out the point.[3] Capacity utilization is one way to confirm the small scale of developing country firms. Multinationals from the advanced countries on the average operated at only 26 percent of their capacity, whereas foreign investors from other developing countries operated at 48 percent. The role of scale is verified when the outputs of the plants of various nationalities are compared. The size of an average plant owned by an industrialized country parent was more than twice the size of an average plant owned by a developing country parent within the same industry.

In another study, Lecraw compared a group of foreign investors from Southeast Asian countries with multinationals from wealthy countries. He calculated index numbers to measure relative size for each industry, with the largest firm in the industry assigned the number 100. The size of the subsidiaries from Southeast Asian parents averaged 46; the counterparts from the industrialized countries averaged 109.[4]

A study of Taiwan's exports of capital equipment provided additional support for the contention that firms in developing countries innovate small-scale technology.[5] It demonstrated that Taiwan's advantage in such exports appears in the sale of equipment for small-scale plants.

In the interviews for this study, managers were asked how the sizes of their home plant and their subsidiaries would compare to the size of typical plants in an industrialized country. The typical answer was "smaller." The following data illustrate the sizes of the subsidiaries of firms that were interviewed. Hong Kong managers reported, as evidence, the number of looms for five overseas subsidiaries to be 3,000, 1,920, 440, 250, and 200. One Argentine firm indicated that it had 169, 240 and 168 looms in its three Brazilian mills.[6] Hong Kong firms reported the number of spindles for seven spinning subsidiaries to be 110,000,

Table 3.2
Average investment in manufacturing subsidiaries in Indonesia (1967–1976)

Home of investor	Average total investment (× $1,000)
Chinese in Hong Kong, Singapore, and Taiwan	2,722
Other Southeast Asian countries	960
Other developing countries	3,935
Japan	5,687
United States	2,403
United Kingdom	1,189
Other industrialized countries	2,063

Source: Calculated from data on realized projects from the Indonesian Investment Board.

100,000, 40,000, 23,000, 16,000, 14,000, 10,000, 10,000.[7] Two Indian firms reported 30,000 and 20,160 spindles in their subsidiaries. The Argentine firm had 14,700, 29,800, and 11,500 spindles in its foreign factories.[8] by the standards of the industrialized countries, these are almost all small plants.[9]

More evidence of the comparatively small size of factories owned by foreign investors from developing countries was provided by foreign investors in Nigeria and Indonesia. In Nigeria, textile plants owned by nationals from other developing countries were, in most cases, smaller than the subsidiaries owned by European, American, or Japanese parents.[10] In Indonesia, factories for flashlight batteries show a similar pattern. A Singapore-owned factory (with Taiwanese technicians) had a capacity of 12 million batteries per year on a one-shift basis. In contrast, an American-owned factory in Indonesia could produce more than 65 million batteries in the same period.[11]

Aggregate data are more difficult to analyze but tend to support the same conclusions. Consider Indonesia, for which a great deal of information was available about investors of various national origins. The Indonesian data suggest that there might not be any consistent differences between the subsidiaries of parents from developing countries and those from advanced countries (table 3.2). However, the overall figures are misleading. A disproportionate number of developing country subsidiaries are for food processing, and they are among the largest projects of developing countries. When one examines the capital investment by industry, a more consistent pattern emerges. Out of 8 two-digit SIC (Standard Industrial Classification) industries with both developing country and industrialized country investors, the average developing country subsidiary has a smaller investment in 6 industries. (The exceptions are in "food, beverages, and tobacco" and in "stone, glass and similar products," which contain only 2 developing country projects.) In the textile and paper products industries, the average developing country subsidiary is considerably less than half the size of its competitors from industrialized countries. In the remaining cases, the difference is at least 30 percent. When the industries are broken down to the three-digit level, the results are similar. Out of 14 industries with 2 or more subsidiaries of each type of parent, the average subsidiary of a parent from another developing country is smaller in 11 cases. The exceptions are all in food and beverages, where market size is probably not a major constraint in the choice of technology.

There is a substantial risk that differences in capital-labor ratios of the two types of investors could cause the figures to be misleading, as factories with smaller total investment may actually have larger output. To account for this possibility, the plants were compared in terms of capacity of production. Unfortunately, output data were not available for Indonesia. If the employment figures were also smaller for the developing country subsidiaries, then one could feel confident in claiming that the plants were indeed smaller. Unfortunately, the data are not thoroughly convincing. In 15 of the 22 three-digit SIC industries, firms from other developing countries had fewer employees than their advanced country competitors; but the remaining 7 had more.

Although the analysis of such data lends some support to the contention that foreign investors from developing countries have smaller subsidiaries than advanced country firms, a completely convincing case cannot be built without output data. Fortunately, data reported from other countries and the interviews provided strong support for the contention that the two types of investors do build plants of very different sizes.

To be sure, the small-scale technologies used in the foreign subsidiaries of developing country parents were not always those in use in the home plants at the time the investments were made. As wage rates have risen in Hong Kong, for example, labor-intensive machinery appropriate to conditions in Hong Kong a few years earlier has been replaced with more automated equipment, and some of the old machinery has been exported to various affiliates. A complete plant was, for instance, moved to Ghana for textile manufacture. In 1979, a Brazilian bicycle manufacturer had a large-scale factory at home but established a small-scale subsidiary in Bolivia. Managers pointed out that the capacity of the new Bolivian plant was comparable to that of the parent company in Brazil only ten years earlier. Although the Brazilian firm's small-scale technology was outdated at home, in the small Bolivian market it was quite appropriate[12] and not easily available from the advanced countries where such techniques had been long forgotten.

Characteristics of Small-Scale Technology

The most striking characteristic of the technology developed by firms in response to small markets is its labor intensity. India's small-scale sugar mills, for example, employ about three times the workers and a half or a third the capital for the same volume as a mill from an advanced country.[13]

The pattern is similar for the firms examined in this study. Capital-labor ratios for subsidiaries of parents from developing countries with those of subsidiaries of parents from industrialized countries offer the simplest kind of comparison.[14] In Indonesia, the first group uses, on average, only $8,500 of capital for each worker employed; the second group uses $16,300. (Table 3.3 breaks down the data further by nationality of investor.) The striking differences do not result from any special characteristics of Chinese firms, which are very important in Indonesia. It is apparent that investors from developing countries, Chinese or not, use more labor-intensive techniques than do investors from the advanced countries.

Such gross comparisons of capital-labor ratios are quite dangerous, as the observed differences could result from differences in industries in which the various investors are found. Developing country firms might be attracted to industries that are inherently more labor-intensive than those that attract firms from the advanced countries. A breakdown of investment by industry, therefore, allows a more careful comparison of firms originating from different countries. When the original Indonesian industry classifications are used, eight two-digit industries contain subsidiaries of parents from both developing and industrialized countries, and in all eight, the capital-labor ratios of the plants with parents from other developing countries are lower than those of their counterparts from the industrialized countries. In only one case (food and beverages) was the ratio for developing country firms more than 65 percent of the ratio for subsidiaries of firms from the industrialized

Table 3.3
Capital-labor ratios in manufacturing subsidiaries in Indonesia (1967–1976)

Home of investor	Average capital-labor ratios (× $1,000/ worker)	Median capital-labor ratios (× $1,000/worker)
Chinese in Hong Kong, Singapore, and Taiwan	8.3	4.9
Other Southeast Asian countries	8.2	4.5
Other developing countries	10.4	9.4
Japan	18.8	14.1
United States	16.9	10.5
United Kingdom	19.9	10.6
Other industrialized countries	13.2	8.6

Source: Calculated from data on realized projects from the Indonesian Investment Board.

countries. At the three-digit level, the average investors from other developing countries are more labor-intensive in 13 out of the 14 industries that have two or more of each group of firms. The exception again is in food products, where market size provides little constraint on scale.

The results might not arise from differences in technology but from differences in investments for building, working capital, or other assets. The figures for investment in machinery per employee, however, show a pattern similar to that for total investment per worker. The developing country firms invest less in machinery for each job created (table 3.4). These differences are only slightly less striking than the differences in overall capital-labor figures. In five of the eight industries, a comparison of the value of machinery per worker for the firms from other developing countries and the firms from industrialized countries indicates less difference than do the figures for total capital invested per worker.

An understanding of why the two measures differ slightly is not critical at this point, but the differences should not be surprising. Total investment reflects building and working capital as well as machinery. One might argue that a labor-intensive factory would require a larger building to house the greater number of workers. The observed results could arise from either of two sources. One possibility is that investors from developing countries spend less on building than do their industrialized counterparts. Another possible explanation of the pattern

Table 3.4
Machinery investment per worker in manufacturing subsidiaries in Indonesia
(1967–1976)

Home of investor	Average machinery investment ($\times$ \$1,000/worker)
Chinese in Hong Kong, Singapore, and Taiwan	4.42
Other Southeast Asian countries	2.92
Other developing countries	4.89
Japan	8.14
United States	5.37
United Kingdom	5.34
Other industrialized countries	7.14

Source: Calculated from data on realized projects from the Indonesian Investment Board.

is that the developing country firms invest less in working capital. The fact that the Indonesian data show fixed assets as a slightly higher percentage of total investment for the investors from developing countries suggests that this might indeed be the case. One could argue that labor-intensive factories need more working capital than would capital-intensive plants because of the need to meet regular wage bills. One could also argue that such factories can run with smaller inventories and thus need less working capital. On this point, one can only speculate, particularly since the Indonesian data come from official application forms in which working capital could only be estimated. My own guess is that firms from developing countries invest less in buildings and have a slight tendency to underestimate the required working capital when they apply for investment permits.

The main point, that the labor intensity of technology used by foreign investors from developing countries is high, is strongly supported by rather sophisticated analysis of Thai data.[15] Since output data were available for that country, Lecraw was able to estimate production functions for 12 four-digit industries. The results effectively demonstrate that foreign investors from other developing countries use more labor-intensive technology than either Thai firms or foreign investors from industrialized countries.

Another major difference that distinguishes the projects of foreign investors from developing countries from those of local firms in their host countries and those of the multinationals from the industrialized countries is flexibility. Flexibility was emphasized quite explicitly by the manager of a Hong Kong textile firm with subsidiaries in Indonesia and Malaysia, who said that the operations "have to be flexible to weave many kinds of textiles and spin many kinds of yarn. We don't make something and then sell it." The implication was that advanced country multinationals make a small variety of products and then devote their efforts to convincing consumers to accept the standardized versions, while his firm responds to market niches by providing a wide range of products.

Since one specialized model or version of a product is unlikely to have a sufficiently large market in developing countries to keep typical machines fully occupied, machines are designed or chosen for their flexibility. Thus, Packages Limited of Pakistan carefully studied the downtime involved in product changeovers for various kinds of European machinery used for making paper packages and used these studies to select equipment that minimizes the costs of short runs of many products. Similarly, a Hong Kong appliance maker selected sheet metal working equipment that can be used to produce various models of both stoves and refrigerators. The manager of a Hong Kong textile firm with spinning facilities in Indonesia explained that using "small package spindles" was more labor-intensive than the usual spindles, requiring more loading and unloading, but was "more flexible." A manager from a Southeast Asian pharmaceutical firm that makes as many as 400 products at home and 50–100 products in the company's foreign subsidiaries reported that the plants "must use the same equipment for many products."

In their efforts to design flexible plants, firms from developing countries occasionally build a special kind of excess capacity into their factories. The plant design includes extra machines required to produce special models or versions of the basic products, even though those machines may stay idle much of the year. The Hong Kong textile manager just quoted explained that he did "not expect every piece of equipment to be used all the time." Packages Limited had a simple machine for making paper cups that was used only occasionally, since the principal customer for paper cups, the Pakistani national airline, did not order enough to keep the machine fully occupied. Nevertheless, paper cups and similar products were needed to fill out the company's line and keep other machinery busy.

In some cases, the design of a flexible, small-scale plant depends largely on knowing well equipment available from a large number of suppliers in the industrialized countries. A German machine for one step may be combined with an Italian one for the next operation. A few firms in the developing countries have made the large investment required to learn about a wide range of such equipment. They not only have collected specifications but have tried the equipment for reliability and know the availability of spare parts. Once acquired, such knowledge is useful in other small markets.

The special knowledge possessed by some companies from developing countries is quite extensive. One firm I interviewed had drawn up a list of suppliers for various pieces of equipment. The list covered a wide range of European suppliers and included the capacity and cost of the equipment and the set-up time required to adjust the equipment to other kinds of output. The supplying firms were evaluated according to their delivery and service records; the machines, according to their needs for maintenance. This was invaluable information for competition with firms in other countries.

To meet the special needs of small-scale manufacture, a number of developing countries have manufactured their own machinery. When special machinery from the home country was used by the firms interviewed, it was usually made by the firm that operated it, not by specialist machinery manufacturers. Typically, a firm started at home with all, or almost all, imported equipment. As the company replaced imported machinery or expanded, the experience gained by its technicians enabled it to supply more of the technology and machinery internally.[16] Eventually, some of this machinery was used abroad. For instance, the original plant of Packages Limited in Pakistan began with equipment acquired in Europe. Spare parts, however, were expensive by the time they reached Pakistan, and lead times in acquiring them were such that repairs could not be made quickly. Moreover, some of the original European equipment was second-hand and quite old; parts for this machinery were not easily available even in Europe. Since local shops were unable to make needed parts quickly and reliably, the firm established its own machine shop and foundry. The shop had excess capacity as long as it supplied only spares, so the shop operators began to experiment with modifications to the original machinery that might improve its performance. Such modifications in some cases increased flexibility by generally decreasing set-up time. Gradually, the shop began to copy the imported machines, but with modifications that were useful for short runs of many products. Eventually, the shop was producing a number of machines largely of its own design, with special features in response to local problems. As Packages Limited ventured outside of Pakistan, it provided its foreign affiliates with machinery of its own manufacture.[17]

Since U.S. studies have discovered the importance of a close link between the user of capital equipment and the supplier for successful innovation,[18] it should perhaps not be surprising that the adapted equipment in developing countries is so often made "in-house." If innovations were undertaken by firms that are first and foremost machinery manufacturers, they would probably be involved in some of the investments uncovered in this study. To sell innovative machines abroad, little-known machinery manufacturers from developing countries might well have to take equity positions in facilities that would use the machinery. The infrequency of foreign investments by firms that were primarily machinery manufacturers suggests that they have not been as innovative as some of the equipment users who felt pressing needs for changes in the machinery.

Investors from developing countries obtain a considerable amount of their equipment from their home nations. For this study, data were available on the source of machinery for 151 subsidiaries; 122 subsidiaries imported machinery from their home country (or, occasionally, another developing country). A study of Taiwanese firms found that more than 30 percent of their foreign investment in nontrade activities was made up of Taiwanese machinery.[19] The Indians are particularly likely to use equipment from home. Given the Indian government requirements that Indian firms use Indian machinery overseas, the finding is not surprising. Firms from other developing countries bring a quarter of their machinery from their home countries. Although this fraction is smaller than the fraction of home machinery used by investors from the advanced countries, it is still a large number given the small amount of machinery manufactured and exported by developing countries. Table 3.5 shows the sources of various foreign investors in Thailand.

A striking fact that appears in table 3.5 is that a quarter of the machinery of developing country investors is made in Thailand, which is more than even local investors use. Thus, the foreign investors have a high propensity to use local machinery as well as local materials in Thailand. My impression from interviews is that locally produced machinery is usually made to order to designs supplied by the parent.

Machines newly manufactured at home or in the host country and carefully selected new machinery from the industrialized countries do

Table 3.5
Source of machinery in manufacturing firms in Thailand (1962–1974)

Home of investor	Source of machinery (%)						
	United States	Europe	Japan	India	Other developing countries	Thailand	Total (%)
United States	51	25	16	0	0	8	100
Europe	20	57	13	0	0	10	100
Japan	6	4	80	0	0	10	100
India	4	10	8	45	8	25	100
Other developing countries	7	8	30	5	25	25	100
Thailand	30	27	26	2	25	13	100

Source: Donald Lecraw, "Choice of Technology in Low-Wage Countries," unpublished doctoral dissertation in business economics, Harvard University, 1976. Original data from Thai Investment Board and interviews.

not exhaust the sources of small-scale equipment for foreign investment by firms from the developing countries. Second-hand machinery provides an important alternative.[20] In most cases, such machinery was produced in an industrialized country, but when the market there was smaller or before technological change had increased the optimal scale for the high-wage country.[21]

The interviews for this study identified a large number of subsidiaries that operated some second-hand machinery. Machinery formerly used in Hong Kong, for example, has been located all over Southeast Asia and as far away as West Africa.

In most cases, old machinery is more labor-intensive and flexible than new equipment. In the textile industry, for instance, spinning equipment of 1950 vintage has roughly half the output per man-hour of 1968 equipment.[22] To be sure, occasionally newer machinery is more flexible; recent innovations in electronic controls for carpet weaving have increased flexibility, according to the manager of one firm interviewed. Although applications of electronics to machinery may make this kind of case more common, in the late 1970s it seemed that "old" usually implied "flexible."

In sum, foreign investors from developing countries obtain their equipment from a range of sources, but regardless of the source, the machinery that is selected is usually flexible, labor-intensive, and suited for relatively small-scale manufacture.

Low Overheads

Low overheads give many developing country firms a strength that supports their ability to manufacture at small volumes with low unit costs. The savings in overhead costs derive largely from the low salaries that such firms pay to managers and technicians and partly from the small expenditures on buildings.

Hong Kong-based foreign investors in one study reported that they consider lower costs for managerial and technical staff as their most important advantage over other multinationals.[23] The possible contribution to competitive position of low expatriate salaries is suggested by a study of U.S.-based multinationals that reported that expatriate costs represented 4 to 20 percent of the pretax profits of all international operations.[24] Since the number of expatriates in a subsidiary is not proportional to the size of sales, the costs would be an even larger percentage of profits for small operations in developing countries

The salaries paid to managers and technicians of the foreign subsidiaries of firms from developing countries appear strikingly low compared to those paid by a multinational from an industrialized country. An Indian firm reported paying a department head between $350 and $700 a month at home, with no significant premiums for overseas assignments. A Hong Kong textile firm reported salaries for its engineers in Indonesia of about $1,000 to $1,200 per month, considerably less than that of a U.S. or European engineer stationed in Southeast Asia. Many of the managers and technicians from developing countries do not take their families with them on overseas assignments, even when the assignment is a year or more. This is especially true for Pakistani and Taiwanese firms. The result is more savings for the firm.

Two additional characteristics of compensation for managers are, in some cases, important in saving overheads for the firms in this study. In a number of Hong Kong enterprises, managers receive a significant part of their income in the form of a bonus, which is large only if the subsidiary does well. For such firms, the fixed costs associated with expatriate managers are comparatively low. In addition, the managers are, in many cases, relatives of the owners of the parent firm. For Chinese firms particularly, the relatives would be drawing a certain amount of income out of the enterprise even if they were not managing a foreign subsidiary. Thus, their incremental cost to the enterprise is small.

Why developing country investors spend less than multinationals from advanced countries on building and operate in more cramped quarters is less apparent, but this fact has been observed before.[25] The traveler in the developing world can hardly avoid being struck by the attractive, modern buildings of the advanced country multinationals. In many cases, they are virtual carbon copies of plants at home. In Indonesia, the Jakarta Coca-Cola bottling plant is, for example, hardly distinguishable from a Coca-Cola bottling plant in a medium-size U.S. city, even down to having windows for pedestrians to watch the automatic bottling equipment.[26] The plant is spacious and attractive and expensive. On the other hand, the Singapore-based F&N bottling plant in Jakarta is clean, sturdy, and seemingly quite adequate to the task but simple and somewhat crowded. Some of the Chinese-owned plastic sandal factories in Indonesia are more austere. Many operate from little more than rudimentary sheds, jammed with workers, inventory, and equipment. The manager may have only a tiny cubicle in a corner, filled with files and papers. Data on buildings in Mauritius and the Philippines indicate the same pattern.[27]

The reasons for the different approaches to building probably lie in the role that image plays in the marketing strategies of firms from different areas. For certain multinationals from rich countries, such as Coca-Cola, image is important, and buildings play at least some part in maintaining that image. As will later become apparent, image is second to price and cost in the strategies of most foreign investors from developing countries.

The savings that can accrue from low overhead add up. The Thai data show adminstrative expenses to be only 5 percent of sales for foreign investors from developing countries. For the traditional multinationals, they amount to 14 percent.[28]

Exploiting the Advantages

The firm that ventures abroad from a developing country has two principal types of competition: firms indigenous to the country in which they are investing and multinationals from the industrialized nations. If the advantage of the firm from another developing country lies in small-scale manufacture, a potential indigenous competitor would have to develop similar skills or work out some kind of arrangement to obtain the skills from a foreign enterprise. To develop the skills at home, the potential competitor must incur costs similar to those already incurred by the foreign firm. If the equipment is designed and produced by the firm, the development costs are likely to be high. If the technology involves the gathering of machinery from a number of countries, the expenses involved in searching out such sources will be significant. If the machinery is second-hand, the task is to find reliable sources. Even when the potential competitor is knowledgeable about suppliers, the risks associated with purchase appear great, and the variance in performance of second-hand equipment is large.[29] The search for a reliable dealer is likely to involve some costly mistakes. Moreover, in most cases, the firm that has experience with small-scale technology has lower costs that have resulted from using technology over a period of time. A potential competitor must incur the costs of acquiring experience before it can be on equal footing with the foreign firm. Whatever the nature of the costs required of the potential indigenous competitor, they are almost certainly greater than those involved in transferring the foreign firm's skills to the potential competitor's country.

A multinational from the United States, Europe, or Japan could, it would seem, apply its formidable skills to scale down production and develop technology that is most suitable for developing countries. Through its large network, the multinational enterprise could spread the development costs over many plants. In fact, multinationals have usually not devoted their resources to down-scaling. Rather, they have preferred to concentrate on advanced technology or on marketing skills that enable them to avoid worrying about production costs. Most see their comparative advantages in fields other than small-scale manufacture. Even if they were to develop the know-how and experience, as some have attempted (such as Philips of The Netherlands),[30] they would still be saddled with high overhead costs not assumed by the investor from a developing country.

The strategies of a number of multinationals from the advanced countries have been just the opposite. Some familiar firms have built or preserved a competitive advantage in their international businesses by integrating operations across national boundaries. In some cases, such integration has allowed the enterprises to obtain low production costs through sheer scale of manufacture. In Europe, Ford Motor Company has, since the 1960s, designed its automobiles so that certain components are common to models offered in different markets. Common components are produced for all of Europe in large, specialized plants in one or two places. The German and British operations, for example, trade certain engines and transmissions that they produce in large volumes. Another approach in the search for economies of scale is to specialize plants by models of the final product rather than by parts. Volkswagen, for example, has produced the "Safari" in Mexico ("The Thing" in the U.S. market) for several of its overseas markets, even though some of those markets have plants that produce other models of Volkswagen.

In some truly exceptional cases, similar integration strategies appear from time to time among firms from the developing countries. A Peruvian firm, Pan Americana, produced television programs in several countries. The same programs could be used in different markets; moreover, there were opportunities to obtain certain kinds of talent cheaply in one country and other kinds in other countries. To take advantage of the opportunities, Pan Americana operated in Argentina, Puerto Rico, Venezuela, and cities of the continental United States with a large Spanish-speaking population. The international business ground to a halt only when the Peruvian government restricted the firm's activities and eventually acquired control. Similarly, Televisa, a large Mexican television firm, established operations in Los Angeles and elsewhere in the United States.[31] The firm is able to use the same programs in Mexico and for the Latin American community in Los Angeles.

In conventional manufacturing, no developing country firms were encountered that had integrated operations across borders. Rather than attempting to emulate firms from the richer countries, the developing country investors stuck by their skill in small-scale manufacture. The reader should not, however, be misled. The factories are neither primitive nor tiny. They are not the rural, almost handicraft industries of Ghandi. And, as will become apparent, running them demands a great deal of management and technical skill.

4   Local Procurement and Special Products as Competitive Advantages

Although adaptation of technology to the small scale required for developing countries is widespread among Third World firms, it hardly exhausts their innovative activities. Other technological developments have given certain enterprises from developing countries advantages that they can exploit abroad, and these advantages stem from special conditions in the firms' home countries.

Use of Local Resources

One such condition is the chronic balance of payments difficulties that have plagued many developing countries. Their governments have responded, in many cases, with severe controls on imports, sometimes to discourage local consumption and sometimes to encourage local manufacture of what had been imported. The resulting high prices for imported products has encouraged local entrepreneurs to begin manufacturing many goods that had previously come from abroad. Such controls provided the incentive for the creation of many of the parent firms in this study. But the influence of import controls has not stopped with the establishment of a factory to manufacture a final product that had been imported, for the factory itself faces a need to import materials and components.

In the advanced countries, where manufacturing technologies have usually originated, the design of end products reflects the wide availability of high-quality materials and special items in the industrialized markets. Special steels, custom-made threaded parts, and an unending array of other special materials and components are readily obtainable and of predictable quality as a result of the scale of demand from industrial firms and the skills available in the richer countries.

In developing countries, a local manufacturer needing specialized inputs has a problem. The producer may need steel products, but if there is a steel plant in the country, its output is likely to be of the most widely demanded sorts. Special steels must come from abroad. Similarly, regular nuts and bolts may be readily available from local suppliers, but special threads and shapes are difficult to come by locally. Moreover, with little competition, local suppliers often produce materials and components of low or unpredictable quality. Imports may be available, but the policies designed to discourage foreign exchange expenditures and promote industrialization are likely to make them very expensive.[1] Moreover, the lead times for foreign orders (or for special manufacture locally, for that matter) are likely to be long.

To diminish the need for special inputs associated with technology imported from the industrialized countries, firms in the developing world might search out ways to substitute locally available inputs. Indeed, they do. The importance of this task is pointed out in a study showing that most of the R&D of Indian firms (even the largest) "originated in the problem of manufacturing standard products out of the non-standard raw materials. . . ."[2] Packages Limited, a Pakistan firm interviewed for this study, had an extensive program of developing local materials. The firm replaced imported adhesives, lacquers, linseed oil, and alum with substitutes that it manufactured locally. Further, the company helped local firms to develop adequate quality soapstone, chalk, and silicate for its plant.[3]

Once firms have learned to substitute locally available materials and components for specialized inputs, they can use that know-how in other developing countries where manufacturers would face similar problems. For example, in cooperation with The Technology Consulting Centre, a Ghanaian entrepreneur came up with a paper glue made from cassava starch and alkali extracted from plantain peels. After capturing a large part of the Ghanaian market for glue, the firm reached an agreement to manufacture the product in the Ivory Coast, where cassava and plantains are also abundant.

Latin American firms also have innovated to make use of local raw materials. A Brazilian steel firm has led in the development of a technology to use charcoal instead of coking coal in the steel reduction process. The innovation was designed to reduce the firm's dependence on special metal-grade coal that was not available in Brazil.[4] Similarly, a Mexican firm has developed (with U.S. involvement) an efficient direct reduction technology that uses gas. The Brazilian and Mexican firms are now transferring technology to other developing countries that do not have a local supply of coking coal.

The advantages of firms from developing countries in this kind of innovation appear not to be limited to nations with strict import controls or even to innovations made at home and exported. The long lead times and difficulty in obtaining special inputs from abroad seem to have left their mark on a number of firms even in the open economies of East Asia. For example, when a paint manufacturer from an Asian island joined with a U.S. multinational for the manufacture of paint in a Southeast Asian country, a conflict developed quite early. The U.S. partner had provided a technician whose job was to supervise the chemicals used in the plant. The Asian partner suggested that local minerals could be used; the technician from the United States insisted that they could not. The dispute finally led to the dismissal of the technician and his replacement by a national of the Asian partner's country. Local minerals, after suitable reformulation of the mixtures, proved quite satisfactory and clearly met the tough quality standards demanded by the U.S. firm whose brand name was being used (and jealously protected by the U.S. partner).

Other examples indicate a related but not identical advantage held by the firm that has innovated at home when it has faced a similar problem abroad. The experience of innovating at home seems to provide managers with the flexibility to find substitute materials in other countries, even if those substitutes differ from what the firm uses at home. Thus, an Indian firm had its Indian labs develop processes for its Mauritius subsidiary to use Mauritius coral sand for cement manufacture. An innovative paper manufacturer from one developing country has experimented abroad with local raw materials that are quite different from what the firm used at home. Thus, the firm that has learned to make paper from rice stalks finds it relatively easy to substitute another plant in some other tropical country for imported softwoods from temperate countries. The critical step seems to be the one that carries the firm away from the materials used in the standard technologies available from the industrialized countries.

Innovations designed to use local materials are so desired by other developing countries that firms are occasionally actively courted by foreign governments or firms to provide their know-how. A Philippine firm, for example, owns an apparently successful technology for producing paper from a mixture of pulpwood that contains a high percentage of tropical hardwoods to substitute for pulp from temperate softwoods. Although many other developing countries have, for some time, been searching for ways of using commercially unattractive woods from their tropical forests for paper manufacture, it seemed that the Philippine firm held a lead over many competitors. Although it had not by 1979 sold its technology or invested in other developing countries, it had been contacted by representatives of other countries seeking the know-how.

Although multinationals from advanced countries may, on occasion, substitute locally available inputs for the inputs to which they are accustomed, Thai data suggest that foreign investors from developing countries use local materials much more frequently.[5] Factories in Thailand belonging to parents from other developing countries imported only 39 percent of their raw materials; subsidiaries of multinationals from the advanced countries imported 76 percent. Even Thai-owned manufacturers had large imports: 65 percent of their materials. The differences among the various kinds of investors could not be explained by differences in the industry mix.

Although local competitors are likely to face pressures for innovation similar to those faced by factories belonging to parents from other developing countries, firms from the richer developing countries benefit from the advantage that comes with having already faced and dealt with the problems. Some have already incurred the costs of developing solutions that can be used directly in poorer countries. Even when the specific knowledge needed for a certain foreign country has not been developed, perhaps because of the special nature of local materials, the firm from a more industrialized developing country has an advantage over a local firm, since it is likely to have had enough experience with similar innovations to do the incremental development of new innovations.

Although multinationals from advanced countries could, and sometimes do, carry out such innovations,[6] there are several reasons why they do not often do so. First, their personnel are typically experienced in the markets of the industrialized countries where such innovations are not necessary. Further, even if the "mind set" of managers were to be changed, it is not clear that the pressures to adapt would be as great for the advanced country multinationals. If the multinational faces less price competition (as this study will suggest is typical), then there is less pressure on managers to innovate to save money.[7] Moreover, the multinational from an advanced country is more likely than developing country firms to be manufacturing its inputs in affiliated factories elsewhere. With captive sources at its disposal, the multinational enterprise as a whole may have lower relevant costs than would a developing country firm that must obtain inputs abroad from unaffiliated enterprises. For the advanced country multinational, the relevant costs are the marginal costs of additional output from its affiliated plants, while the developing country competitor is likely to have to pay full costs. In addition, the multinational might well have some preference for importing from its affiliates to gain the option of manipulating transfer prices on the materials.[8] It may, for example, want to extract profits from a local partner or escape local exchange controls. The desire on the part of the firm from a developing country may be similar, but it cannot exercise that option if it does not have controlled sources of inputs overseas. Finally, advanced country firms are particularly likely to emphasize brand name (as will be evident later) and thus be concerned with producing a product of very standardized quality. Local inputs, with their varying standards, are likely to pose particular problems for such firms.

Ethnic Products

Some interesting investments identified in the research were based on another, rather special kind of advantage. These subsidiaries were established primarily to serve a local community that was related to an ethnic group of the investor's home country. Such projects form a small percentage of the total foreign investments of firms from developing countries but nevertheless account for a significant number of the "upstream" investments, those aimed at industrialized countries. For example, a Hong Kong firm bought a building in Sydney to house a Chinese restaurant and newspaper. Indian firms own Indian restaurants in Britain (at least two) and the United States (at least four).[9]

Many of the "ethnic investments" are within the developing countries and include projects such as the Singapore manufacturers that make Chinese biscuits and noodles in Indonesia and the plant owned by an Indian manufacturer to produce gripe water in Kenya.[10] One group of atypical plants in Indonesia belonging to developing country investors has already been mentioned: food processing facilities. Their advantages did not lie in small-scale or labor-intensive production, according to comparisons with plants owned by advanced country investors, but largely in their ability to produce products for the local Chinese community.

The success of firms that produce ethnic products overseas is a simple matter. It reflects an ability of those firms to manufacture and market products that appeal to people whose tastes are well known to the manufacturer. In some cases, the investing firms bring brand names that are familiar to the local community as well as products that are already known. In fact, such firms account for some of the exceptions to the generalizations made later about the unimportance of product differentiation in the marketing strategies of firms from the developing countries.

In contrast to most of the foreign investors discussed thus far in this book, the competitive edge of the producers of ethnic products seems less likely to be in process than in product. Nevertheless, one still wonders whether Kenyans even know the technology of manufacturing Indian gripe water.

Other Innovations

Simple generalizations fail to describe all the innovations of multi-nationals, whether they come from industrialized countries or from developing countries. As a rule, the Europeans innovated to save capital and raw materials, which were scarce in those economies, but consider the strength of German pharmaceutical firms which seems to have arisen in part from the large market created by the German government's early entry into a national health scheme. Firms in the developing countries have also had a rich history of innovations, not just those suggested by small-scale markets and scarce or expensive inputs. Nevertheless, the innovations have usually been in response to special conditions in the home market.

The early innovation of rice equipment in Thailand provides an example of the variety of innovations by firms in developing countries. Although the original plants for the steam milling of rice were established by westerners, by the last quarter of the nineteenth century local Chinese had gained a great deal of strength. First, they bought western mills, initially hiring foreigners to run them. Soon the Chinese-owned firms began to make their own machinery, originally from sketches of British equipment. About 1890, they pioneered a process for producing white rice that was eventually copied by Europeans.[11] The location of innovation, of course, reflects the importance of rice in the diets of Southeast Asia.

An example from Latin America illustrates other innovative activities that are similar to those of U.S. firms. In response to high labor costs and the large size of many local farms, Argentine enterprises have innovated mechanized agricultural equipment and other farm and food processes and, in fact, built the first corn harvester in the world. Of 33 Argentine exports of plants and civil works between 1973 and 1977, 19 were related to agriculture.[12] Not surprisingly, food and agricultural sectors are heavily represented in Argentine foreign investment as well. Almost 20 percent of the manufacturing subsidiaries of Argentine firms operate in the food industry (SIC 20); the comparable figure for subsidiaries of firms from other developing countries is less than 12 percent.

In many cases, innovations in the developing countries are in response to what would be viewed as hostile environments for products from the industrialized nations. Thus, an Indian firm formulated dyes that were more sun-resistant than those available from the more temperate climates. The innovator found a market for the dyes in other developing countries and eventually set up production facilities outside India. Similarly, in 1979, Brazilians were exporting household appliances to Africa with the claim that they were "Made for the Tropics." The appliances were said to be more resistant to damage from voltage fluctuations and high humidity than were similar products available from Europe and America.[13] The Brazilians were also contemplating overseas production as a response to the requirements of a major importing country that products be manufactured locally. In 1980, a Brazilian automobile maker made U.S. news when it began manufacturing the Gurgel. The specialized vehicles and their accessories were designed for tough road conditions and for jobs that were unusual in the advanced countries, such as rescuing people from wells. The firm was soon to make electric cars and was already providing alcohol-powered Gurgels in response to the shortage and high cost of oil in Brazil. Moreover, the auto's chassis was made of steel-reinforced plastic and fiberglass, a technique very well suited to small-scale manufacture. According to *The New York Times*, 25 percent of the output was being exported, with plants anticipated for Panama and Ecuador.[14]

Level of Technology

Regardless of the type of innovation, the advantages held by firms from developing countries have resulted in a concentration of foreign subsidiaries in industries somewhat different from those in which investors from the advanced countries are located. The turf of the developing country investors is not that of "high-technology" industries.

Table 4.1
Manufacturing investment in Brazil, by intensity and type of technology and
nationality of investors (1979)

Intensity and type of technology	Percentage of investment from other developing countries in each industry	Percentage of investment from industrialized countries in each industry
Low		
Food and beverages	0.7	5.1
Textiles	26.1	3.0
Medium		
Basic metals and products	44.0	10.0
High		
Electrical products	4.1	11.1
Chemicals	9.9	13.9
Machinery	7.8	11.3

Source: Brazilian data from *Buletin do Banco Central do Brasil*, June 1979.
Note: Due to the aggregate level of reporting, only a few industries could be compared.
The classifications are those of Ting (see table 3.3).

For several host countries, data were available that allowed comparisons between foreign investors from other developing countries and foreign investors from the industrialized nations. When the data were available, comparisons were made at a rather detailed industry level (three-digit SIC). Tables 4.1 to 4.6 present data for Brazil, Indonesia, Taiwan, the Philippines, and Mauritius. The resulting patterns show clearly that foreign investors from developing countries were disproportionately represented in industries not characterized by high R&D expenditures in the United States.

Although the varied sources of data make direct comparisons across countries somewhat difficult, the consistency of the pattern is striking. For Brazil, Indonesia, and Taiwan, the comparisons are almost entirely of firms manufacturing for the domestic market. Even in the Philippines and Mauritius, where the comparison is primarily among export-oriented firms, the firms from developing countries are more likely to be in less R&D-oriented industries than their counterparts from the advanced countries.

The comparisons thus far have matched foreign investors from developing countries with all foreign investors from the advanced countries. The differences are particularly striking if the firms from the

Table 4.2
Number of industries (three-digit SIC) with subsidiaries in Indonesia, by R&D expenditures and most significant foreign investors (1967–1976)

Industries' expenditure on R&D as percentage of sales[a]	Number of industries in which firms from other developing countries are the most significant investors[b]	Number of industries in which firms from industrialized countries are the most significant investors[b]
Low (less than 1%)	9	4
Medium (from 1% but less than 2.5%)	2	9
High (2.5% or more)	3[c]	13

Source: Data for realized projects from Indonesian Investment Board.
a. U.S. data.
b. By number of subsidiaries.
c. The industrial inorganic chemicals industry (281 subsidiaries), the plastic materials and synthetic resins, synthetic rubber, synthetics and other man-made fibers industry (282 subsidiaries), and the motor vehicles industry (371 subsidiaries), which contains only one LDC firm.

Table 4.3
Investment and number of foreign manufacturing firms in Taiwan, by technology intensity and nationality of investors

Technology intensity	Investors from United States, Europe, Japan		Investors from other Asian countries	
	Investment ($\times$ $1 million)	Number of subsidiaries	Investment ($\times$ $1 million)	Number of subsidiaries
Low	27.24	94	98.00	320
Medium	166.41	261	105.78	296
High	853.10	486	42.28	173

Source: Wen-Lee Ting, "Transfer of Intermediate Technology by Third-World Multi-nationals," mimeograph, Tatung Institute of Technology, Taiwan, 1979.

Table 4.4
Manufacturing subsidiaries in the Philippines by R&D expenditures and nationality of investors

Industries' (three-digit SIC) expenditure on R&D as percentage of sales[a]	Subsidiaries of other developing countries (1970–1978)		Subsidiaries of United States (1968–1977)	
	Number	%	Number	%
Low (less than 1%)	19	59	49	38
Medium (from 1% but less than 2.5%)	8	25	45	34
High (2.5% or more)	5	16	36	28

Source: Vinod Busjeet, "Foreign Investors from Less Developed Countries," unpublished doctoral dissertation, Harvard Business School, 1980.
a. U.S. data.

Table 4.5
Industries (three-digit SIC) in Mauritius Export Processing Zone, by R&D expenditure and nationality of most significant investors (1970–1978)

Industries' expenditure on R&D as percentage of sales[a]	Number of industries in which firms from other developing countries are the most significant investors[b]	Number of industries in which firms from industrialized countries are the most significant investors[b]	Number of industries in which Mauritius firms are the most significant investors[b]
Low (less than 1%)	7	4	1
Medium (from 1% but less than 2.5%)	0	6	0
High (2.5% or more)	1	2	0

Source: Vinod Busjeet, "Foreign Investors from Less Developed Countries," unpublished doctoral dissertation, Harvard Business School, 1980.
a. U.S. data.
b. By number of subsidiaries or firms.

Table 4.6
Manufacturing subsidiaries in Mauritius Export Processing Zone, by R&D expenditure of industries (three-digit SIC) and nationality of investors (1970–1978)

Industries' (three-digit SIC) expenditure on R&D as percentage of sales[a]	Subsidiaries from other developing countries		Subsidiaries from industrialized countries		Firms from Mauritius	
	Number	%	Number	%	Number	%
Low (less than 1%)	22	88	18	43	11	73
Medium (from 1% but less than 2.5%)	0	0	15	36	4	27
High (2.5% or more)	3	12	9	21	0	0

Source: Vinod Busjeet, "Foreign Investors from Less Developed Countries," unpublished doctoral dissertation, Harvard Business School, 1980.
a. U.S. data.

Table 4.7
Manufacturing subsidiaries in all locations, by R&D expenditures and nationality of investors

Industries' (three-digit SIC) expenditure on R&D as percentage of sales[a]	Subsidiaries from developing countries[b]		Subsidiaries from United States[c]		Subsidiaries from other industrialized countries[c]	
	Number	%	Number	%	Number	%
Low (less than 1%)	537	57.6	2,540	30.2	2,189	35.6
Medium (from 1% but less than 2.5%)	148	15.9	1,286	15.3	795	12.9
High (2.5% or more)	247	26.5	4,573	54.5	3,166	51.5

a. U.S. data.
b. Data bank of this study.
c. Data banks of Harvard Multinational Enterprise Project, U.S. data to 1975, and data from other industrialized countries to 1971.

developing countries are compared with only the "true multinationals" from the advanced countries (table 4.7). The investors from the industrialized countries included only those that qualified as multinationals in Harvard's Multinational Enterprise Project by being very large firms with manufacturing subsidiaries in six or more foreign countries. As will be apparent in other parts of this book, the developing country investors have much more in common with the smaller firms from the advanced countries than they do with the big multinationals.[15]

No matter which comparison one prefers, it is clear, in sum, that the developing country firms innovate in different ways and, frequently, in different industries from firms originating in the industrialized countries. The previous chapter concluded that they have found various ways to manufacture relatively efficiently at small scale. Enterprises from the advanced countries have usually forgotten such technologies and emphasize other skills by the time they go abroad to the Third World. Similarly, firms from developing countries have learned to use locally available inputs to a greater extent than firms from industrialized countries. Further, on occasion Third World firms produce products that are especially appropriate to developing country environments. The characteristics of the different technologies, the different import propensities, and, less frequently, the different products are important factors in weighing the relative benefits of foreign investors from the developing countries and those from the advanced countries. But there are still more differences to be considered.

5   Access to Markets as a Competitive Advantage

Many multinationals have excelled in marketing skills. Coca-Cola, Colgate, and other American trade names are known throughout most of the world. In some cases, mass marketing skills gave American multinationals their principal competitive advantage when they went abroad. Around the turn of the century, U.S.-based firms were strong in selling life insurance in Britain, for example, and their expertise lay in the marketing skills required to package and sell insurance to a large middle-class population.

Marketing know-how has often accompanied technological skills. For mass-produced automobiles, American firms mastered early not only the manufacturing know-how but, equally important, the distribution techniques. They also have learned how to provide the service and software needed to market high-technology items such as computers. Some other American multinationals turned to marketing skills to maintain an edge after their technological skills had been copied. The strengths that enabled them to survive the erosion of their original technological edge came from creating the image of differentiated products, even though the technical attributes of their products could be matched by others.

Some firms have developed a marketing advantage through special relationships at home with a small number of important customers. These relationships can be duplicated only with great difficulty and at considerable cost by would-be competitors. When the customers go abroad, the suppliers may follow. The proven reliability of American suppliers of automobile parts, for example, has placed them in a strong position to set up facilities overseas to supply U.S.-based automobile firms as they establish assembly plants in foreign countries. Some firms in this study had similar advantages.

Another closely related marketing advantage was held by a group of firms that are fairly important sources of foreign investment from

developing countries. These are the firms that have proved their reliability to certain customers in the advanced countries. When those
firms invest in other developing countries, their reputation is an extremely valuable marketing advantage. They are able to export from
their new bases to their old customers.

Trade Name as an Advantage

Unlike many U.S.-based enterprises, relatively few firms from the Third
World have developed strong trade names for their products even at
home. Still fewer have been able to build a successful international
strategy around differentiated products.

One firm that has developed a brand image at home and transferred
its marketing skills to other countries is the famous Philippine brewer,
San Miguel. That firm was founded in 1890 in Manila, using technical
help from individual brewmasters from Germany. Today, the company's
marketing techniques appear to differ little from those of well-known
breweries in North America or Europe. And the San Miguel name is
known internationally. Moreover, the company has established a chain
of breweries outside the Philippines, including one in Hong Kong, one
in Papua New Guinea, and one in Indonesia, and holdings in three
breweries in Spain. The Hong Kong subsidiary has captured a major
share of the local market. In fact, San Miguel bought out Carling's
Hong Kong brewery after that U.S.-owned operation failed. San Miguel's
strategy in Hong Kong and elsewhere appears to depend on producing
a high-quality beer and promoting its name.

The beer market seems to have provided a rather special opportunity
to developing country firms. In contrast to most other industries for
which product differentiation plays a major role, multinational firms
from the industrialized countries are virtually absent from the world
market in this industry. American companies, which are particularly
strong in most such advertising-intensive industries, have relied on a
version of the product that is rather different from the international
standard. The European industry, on the other hand, has the product,
but the industry has been highly fragmented until recently. The few
really large producers, such as Heineken, Tuborg, and Löwenbräu,
have not turned themselves into multinational enterprises; their foreign
sales have been primarily through exports. When they have become
involved in foreign manufacture, it has most often been through technical assistance without the licensing of their well known names. Thus,

one finds ties between Heineken and Indonesia's Bintang Baru (New Star) beer and between Heineken and Ghana's Star beer, but no effort has been made to capitalize on the Heineken name. Only very recently have Tuborg and Löwenbräu licensed the use of their names in the United States. The reluctance of European brewers to use their names in foreign production may have derived from a desire to protect their export markets. Whatever the reason, the absence of multinationals in this market has left a special opportunity for independent firms from developing countries to build names and then international investments based on the names. Although only a few firms have taken up the opportunity, they appear to have been quite successful.

In contrast to the beer firms, soft drink firms from the developing countries have faced the full brunt of international competition from major multinationals with the skills to differentiate their products. At least two, F&N of Singapore and Inca Kola of Peru, have spread abroad and survived in head-on competition against Coca-Cola and Pepsi.

Price has played some role in the strategy of F&N. One author, in describing F&N's strategy, said "The only way for them to survive is to sell their products at lower prices than those carrying American brand names. . . ."[1] In Indonesia in 1972, a locally bottled F&N orange drink sold at retail for about the same price as a much smaller bottle of Fanta, Coca-Cola's product. F&N's bottling costs appeared to be somewhat lower than those of local plants bottling soft drinks with international names. The cost differences derived from F&N's lower investment in building and its more labor-intensive equipment.[2] However, F&N was competing successfully against a number of Indonesian products that sold for still less and may have had even lower costs. The Singapore-based firm seems to have placed itself in a niche in the middle price range by creating a brand image to command a higher price than local, virtually unbranded, products but by relying on price to help it compete with the multinationals.

Inca Kola found a different route to success. First, it entered the Peruvian market more than seventy years ago, before Coca-Cola arrived. Starting with products modeled on British soft drinks (the firm was founded by an expatriate Britisher), it gradually adapted its products to Peruvian tastes, so that it was eventually producing soft drinks that were quite different from what major international competitors offered. For example, its cola drink had a light yellow color.[3] Moreover, its marketing techniques evolved in ways that were particularly suited to a developing country. In Lima, for example, the pedestals on which policemen direct traffic at major intersections are provided by Inca Kola, with appropriate messages painted on them. A multinational soft drink firm from an industrialized country would not have provided to subsidiaries or licensees such a technique in the "standard kit" of marketing programs, from which local bottlers are expected not to depart. One could even imagine that some nationalistic Peruvian governments might have been hesitant to allow such "public property" to be used for advertising "imperialist" Coca-Cola.

Price, on the other hand, was not an effective tool in the Peruvian soft drink market, at least in recent years. Government controls on domestic and foreign soft drinks held prices sufficiently low that there seemed to be little temptation for Inca Kola or others to undercut competitors. In fact, in 1979, Inca Kola's products sold in Peru for the same retail price as those of its international competitors. Indeed, Inca Kola's management complained that international firms were shading prices to the retailers by providing them with free coolers and other material. According to the local firm, the international brands were being subsidized in Peru from earnings abroad. Whatever the facts, Inca Kola's strategy clearly did not rely on low price as a critical weapon in the late 1970s.

By that time, Inca Kola had succeeded elsewhere. In Ecuador, its affiliates reportedly had captured a large share of the market. Inca Kola's products were being bottled in Los Angeles, where the core market for Inca Kola seems to have been made up of immigrant Latin Americans. In Bolivia, Inca Kola was less successful. Apparently there was a lack of appreciation on the part of managers of the difficulty in transferring the firm's principal asset, marketing know-how.

Although relatively few successful foreign investments by developing country firms have developed trade names that played major roles in their foreign investments, San Miguel, F&N, and Inca Kola are not the only examples. Parle's Confectionary seems to be the only important Indian firm that has successfully carried abroad a consumer good for which brand awareness is important. Parle has managed to sell soft drink franchises in Dubai, Kuwait, and Mauritius. It exports its concentrate from Singapore, supposedly because of difficult Indian export formalities. Tata Oil Mills, which is said to have a strong record with branded products in India, provides something of a contrast. When it went to Malaysia with branded products as well as facilities to extract palm oil, it was the latter that accounted for most of its success.[4]

Some firms from developing countries have managed to acquire skills or trade names by combining their efforts with those of a firm from an advanced country. In such cases, the foreign partner has provided the assets lacking in the developing country firm; the firm from the poorer country has brought to the joint venture other resources needed by the enterprise from an industrialized country.

One such joint venture, between an Asian firm and a U.S. multinational, has already been mentioned. The Asian firm went abroad to another Asian country to manufacture paint. The technology for manufacturing simple paints is relatively easy to master, and small-scale manufacture seems to present few problems, although costs may be somewhat high.[5] The plant was designed at home, using Taiwan equipment to produce only 5,000 gallons per month on a one-shift basis. The subsidiary used its own trade name, which had no established reputation and which received little promotion, but the country was virtually closed to western multinationals. When the parent considered a paint project in a more open Asian country, however, the problem of brand name loomed larger. The decision was to combine forces with a multinational from an industrialized country, which could bring a well-known trade name and the skills to promote it. The Asian firm, it seems, contributed knowledge of how to conduct other aspects of business in an Asian environment, labor management and government relations, for example. The U.S. multinational was allowed to design the plant, but the equipment selected was "too big and fancy," according to the Asian partner. It could produce as much as 40,000 gallons per month on a one-shift basis, although in 1979 the limited market size held actual production to 10,000 gallons per month.

Another case demonstrates the possibility that a developing country firm can learn marketing skills from joint ventures and eventually provide the skills itself in other countries. A Hong Kong firm had established a distributorship in Singapore for a Japanese product. After Singapore began to insist on local manufacture in the late 1950s, the Hong Kong and Japanese firms formed a joint enterprise. The Japanese firm provided its well-known trade name and technical know-how, and the Hong Kong firm contributed its familiarity with the Singapore market. The Hong Kong firm adapted the Japanese know-how to small-scale manufacture and eventually introduced its own brand name in Singapore. Some fifteen years later, the Hong Kong firm decided to expand alone in another Asian market. Management determined that it had adequate technical and marketing skills to introduce products with its own brand name from the outset.

Instead of acquiring a name through joint ventures, one developing country firm accomplished the same feat by purchasing a firm based in an industrialized country. Hong Kong's Stelux Manufacturing Company acquired control of Bulova, a U.S. company, in 1976. Stelux sold its equity interest at a loss two years later but retained certain rights to name and distribution outside North America, Italy, South Africa, and Israel.[6] Stelux thus ended up with a well-known name, perhaps at a cost less than that which it would have had to pay if it had decided to acquire the skills to build a reputation for its own name.

Following the Customer

A few firms from developing countries have, like counterparts from the industrialized countries, relied on their relationships with important customers at home to provide access to markets abroad.

One of the earliest cases I discovered of an international firm based in a developing country began its foreign activities with just such an approach. S.I.A.M. di Tella of Argentina set up its Brazilian operations in 1928 to manufacture gasoline pumps for Shell Mex, a British-based oil company that S.I.A.M. di Tella had been supplying in Argentina. In fact, the Brazilian subsidiary of S.I.A.M. di Tella almost failed because Shell Mex underwent a change of management in Brazil soon after the pump plant was established. New management did not approve of the Argentine pump design, and the market for S.I.A.M. di Tella dried up. Brazilian manufacturing operations were begun again some years later, but for different products.[7]

Although this early example did not, in the end, survive on the marketing access that appeared secure at the time of investment, other examples have been more successful. Some Latin American firms have, for example, established good reputations for supplying parts to the local subsidiaries of automobile assemblers from advanced countries. Those suppliers have then obtained favored access to subsidiaries of the same multinationals in other countries.

The Offshore Manufacturers

Another group of firms from developing countries has established subsidiaries abroad to manufacture products for export to customers they were already serving. Virtually all such "offshore" plants have been established to export to customers in the advanced countries.[8] The competitive advantage of the investors vis-à-vis local firms was their access to those customers, a marketing advantage of a kind quite different from heavy advertising but similar to that of the firms that follow their customers. More than forty offshore plants were identified in this study, but the actual number in existence must be several times this figure. Nevertheless, they do not account for a very large fraction of foreign investment from developing countries.

The first wave of offshore investors from developing countries consisted of fifteen Hong Kong textile firms that began production in Singapore in 1963 and 1964 for export. Those investors were invariably firms that already had exported significant amounts of textiles, had well-established contacts with customers in the industrialized countries, and had a previous record of reliability in meeting delivery schedules.

A prospective new exporter from a country with other successful exporters has substantial advantages over a locally owned exporter in a country without established exporting firms in a particular industry. Since buyers from the advanced countries visit their suppliers regularly, a new firm in an exporting country has a chance of establishing contact with a buyer when he calls on one of his regular suppliers. But a potential exporter in a new country is likely to find it difficult to overcome buyers' reluctance to visit a new site, since a buyer would much prefer to stop in a location where there are numerous potential suppliers.[9] Hong Kong and Taiwan are frequent stopovers for buyers; thus, the subsidiary of a Hong Kong or Taiwan parent can rely on the parent's contacts to obtain orders no matter where the subsidiary is located.

Even when buyers do visit a country, a new firm can find it difficult to get business. If customers have had good experiences with past suppliers, they are eager to give them more orders rather than to hand them over to a firm whose reliability is not known. The extensive experience of most foreign investors that export in third countries is evident in table 5.1, which reports on firms in the Philippines and Mauritius. Fifteen of twenty parent firms had more than six years of export experience. The extent of market links is pointed out by the fact that 60 percent of Korean exporters in one survey were represented in at least one foreign country through a branch or an affiliated company.[10] Another 13 percent relied on contacts with Korean or Japanese trading companies.

Table 5.1
Export experience of parent firms from developing countries prior to first foreign investment[a] for export manufacturing subsidiaries in Mauritius and the Philippines (1970–1978)

Country of parent	Number of firms with export experience			
	2–3 years	4–6 years	7–9 years	10 or more years
Hong Kong	3	0	3	5
India	1	0	0	3
Other developing countries	0	1	1	3

Source: Vinod Busjeet, "Foreign Investors from Less Developed Countries," unpublished doctoral dissertation, Harvard Business School, 1980. From interviews.
a. First foreign investment not necessarily undertaken in Mauritius or the Philippines.

Indonesia's experience illustrates the barriers that the lack of market contacts pose for a country that wishes its own firms to enter the export market. By 1971, Hong Kong businesses had submitted at least a dozen applications for permission to produce garments in Indonesia for export. However, the Indonesian authorities held back approval. The reasons for not accepting the Hong Kong firms were complex. Certainly, Indonesian feelings against ethnic Chinese were a significant factor in the government's reluctance to approve the proposed investments. The fear that the required export zones would inevitably allow leakage of duty-free items into the Indonesian economy also played a role. However, the hope that enterprises owned by indigenous Indonesians would take up the opportunity was of major importance. If Chinese firms could be kept out, Indonesian firms would then begin to export garments, it was thought. Faced with the lack of market contacts, Indonesian entrepreneurs failed to take up the opportunities reserved to them by the exclusion of Hong Kong firms. For close to a decade, local firms did not export significant quantities of modern garments but concentrated on the large home market. The Hong Kong firms took their export business elsewhere.

Even though the principal advantage of export firms lies in their access to markets, it is very interesting that even export-oriented plants owned by foreign investors from developing countries are more labor-intensive than their counterparts established by firms from the advanced countries, even when they both face tough price competition. Table 5.2 compares firms in the export zones of Mauritius and the Philippines. The careful reader will note that, unlike the previous comparisons, the

Table 5.2
Capital-labor ratios for manufacturing subsidiaries in Mauritius and Philippines Export
Processing Zone (1970–1978)

Country of investor	Average capital-labor ratio in Mauritius ($\times$ $1,000/worker)	Average capital-labor ratio in Philippines ($\times$ $1,000/worker)
Other developing countries	2.1	1.5
Industrialized countries	4.4	9.3

Source: Vinod Busjeet, "Foreign Investors from Less Developed Countries," unpublished
doctoral dissertation, Harvard Business School, 1980. Assembled from data provided by
Mauritius government.

industry was not held constant in the construction of this table. Given
the propensity of developing country firms to invest in industries that
are inherently more labor-intensive, this could be a serious omission.
A breakdown of investments by four-digit SIC code, however, confirmed
the labor intensity. In five out of seven industries, the developing country
firms are more labor-intensive, and this is true when labor intensity is
measured by the capital employed per worker, by value added per
employee, or electricity consumed per employee.

There are differences among the offshore plants established by firms
from developing countries. In Mauritius the subsidiaries of developing
country firms are more similar to those with parents from industrialized
countries than are those in the Philippines. Indian firms, more heavily
represented in Mauritius, seem to place more emphasis on product
differentiation than do Hong Kong firms that operate in the Philippines
and Mauritius.

Most export-oriented firms from developing countries, however, are
similar to their counterparts that serve local markets in that they have
a high propensity to use second-hand equipment. In the Philippine
and Mauritius subsidiaries (mostly export-oriented), 69 percent of the
firms used some second-hand equipment. In 38 percent of the cases,
such equipment accounted for 60 percent or more of all equipment
installed. Hong Kong firms were particularly likely to have second-
hand machinery.

In sum, although the principal competitive advantage of the export
firms is a marketing one, they are in other ways quite similar to other
international manufacturing firms from developing countries.

Price as a Marketing Tool

The soft drink firms, breweries, exporters, and other firms just described account for only a small fraction of the foreign investors from developing countries. Most investors from developing countries are quite unlike the American multinationals that have been so skilled in creating the image of differentiated products, in controlling distribution channels, in providing service, or even in building a strong reputation with a few customers. Most foreign investors from the Third World rely heavily on one marketing tool, price. This propensity is evident in the export strategies as well as in the foreign investments of firms from developing countries. Indian manufactured products, for example, have been regularly sold in export markets at a discount under similar products exported to the same markets from industrialized countries. More important, the discounts were larger for products with greater "marketing requirements." When Indian firms have exported products that must compete with brand names and service, they have tended to sell them at low prices. Thus, steel bars and tubes from India carried only a small discount in foreign markets, while sewing machines and bicycles were sold at 20 to 30 percent below the price of European exports.[11]

When a firm from a developing country invests in production facilities abroad, it tends to follow a marketing strategy similar to that of the Indian exporters. Its technology enables it to produce at low cost in other developing countries, and the resulting savings from manufacturing are used to cut prices rather than increase advertising or improve marketing techniques.

The typical strategy is evident in data covering subsidiaries located in Mauritius and the Philippines. Firms in those countries belonging to developing country parents were asked what elements of marketing they emphasized in their strategies. The results, reported in table 5.3, indicate clearly an emphasis on price. The answers are backed by the firms' reports on their weak efforts to develop brand names and by their low advertising expenditures.

Comparative data are available from other sources. One study covered 23 firms from developing countries and 130 multinationals from the advanced countries. The multinationals from the industrialized nations spent, on the average, significantly more on advertising than did the foreign investors from developing countries. The firms from developing countries operated with lower margins, as expected.[12] The same researcher collected data in Thailand. Advertising and selling expenses

Table 5.3
Emphasis of marketing strategy of subsidiaries of parents from other developing
countries in Mauritius and the Philippines (1970–1978)

Elements of marketing	Number of firms serving primarily export markets (24 firms)	Number of firms serving mix of local and export markets (24 firms)
Price	20	7
Distribution		
Reliable, timely delivery	7	2
Availability of parts and sales service	1	0
Effective use of distribution network	0	1
Product		
High quality	2	2
Width of product line	1	2
Promotion		
Advertising and brand name	0	3

Source: Vinod Busjeet, "Foreign Investors from Less Developed Countries," unpublished
doctoral dissertation, Harvard Business School, 1980. Data from interviews.
Note: Since firms may emphasize more than one element of the marketing mix, column
totals may exceed number of firms in sample.

were reported to average 3 percent of sales for investors from other
developing countries (and for Thai firms) but 8 percent for the multinationals from the industrialized countries.[13] Data for Mauritius and
the Philippines indicated that only 6 (of 24) firms made an effort to
develop brand names. As in Thailand, most spent little on advertising
(table 5.4). For India, data were available only on the parent firms'
expenditures for advertising and selling expenses. More than half spent
2 percent or less of sales on these marketing costs. Only 5 (of 41) firms
spent as much as 6 percent; 22 spent 2 percent or less. The Indian
interviews suggest that when branding is very important, the Indian
firm has typically entered into collaboration with a multinational from
Europe or the United States to obtain the required skills. The terms of
collaboration sometimes restrict the use of the brand names outside
India, thus effectively blocking the use of the names to build multinationals.

The differences in marketing expenditures between developing country firms and traditional multinationals in third countries are partly the

Table 5.4
Advertising expenditures of manufacturing subsidiaries in the Philippines and
Mauritius of parents from other developing countries (1970–1978)

Advertising expenditures as a percentage of sales of the subsidiary	Number of firms serving primarily export markets	Number of firms serving mix of local and export markets
Low (less than 1%)	19	5
Medium (from 1% but less than 2%)	1	0
High (2% or more)	0	3

Source: Vinod Busjeet, "Foreign Investors from Less Developed Countries," unpublished
doctoral dissertation, Harvard Business School, 1980. Data from interviews.

result of the fact that the two types of enterprises invest in a somewhat
different mix of industries. In Indonesia and Mauritius, for example,
firms from other developing countries are disproportionately represented
in industries that are characterized by low advertising expenses in the
United States (tables 5.5 and 5.6). In the Philippines, the pattern is
similar if one considers only the firms producing for the local market
(table 5.7). The different industry mix is particularly apparent if the
developing country firms are compared with the advanced country
multinationals that have manufacturing operations in six or more foreign
countries. In table 5.8, it is clear that the multinationals are more likely
to be in industries where advertising is important.

One can correct for the industry mix. For those industries in which
firms from other developing countries were dominant in Indonesia,
the average expenditure for advertising was 0.8 percent of sales in the
United States; for those industries in which advanced country firms
were the more important, advertising was 1.9 percent of sales in the
United States.

It would be a mistake to think that foreign investors from developing
countries only rarely invest in marketing-intensive industries alongside
their advanced country counterparts. The major point, however, is that
even when the firms are in the same industry, the marketing strategies
of developing country and advanced country investors usually differ.

That firms from developing countries can compete on a price basis
in certain industries can be quite surprising. For example, a price-cutting
strategy for household detergents would appear to hold little promise
of a large market share in the United States or western Europe, but

Table 5.5
Advertising expenditures of industries (three-digit SIC) from developing and industrialized countries with subsidiaries in Indonesia (1967–1976)

Industries' expenditure on advertising as a percentage of sales[a]	Number of industries in which firms from other developing countries are the most significant investors[b]	Number of industries in which firms from industrialized countries are the most significant investors[b]
Low (less than 1%)	7	9
Medium (from 1% but less than 2%)	1[c]	3
High (2% or more)	1[c]	7

Source: Data for realized projects from Indonesian Investment Board.
a. U.S. data.
b. By number of subsidiaries.
c. Industries with only one investor from a developing country.

Table 5.6
Advertising expenditures of manufacturing firms in Mauritius Export Processing Zone (1970–1978)

Industries' (three-digit SIC) expenditure on advertising as percentage of sales[a]	Firms from other developing countries		Firms from industrialized countries		Firms from Mauritius	
	Number of subsidiaries	%	Number of subsidiaries	%	Number of firms	%
Low (less than 1%	24	96	29	69	13	86.67
Medium (from 1% but less than 2%)	0	0	4	9.5	1	6.67
High (2% or more)	1	4	9	21.5	1	6.67

Source: Vinod Busjeet, "Foreign Investors from Less Developed Countries," unpublished doctoral dissertation, Harvard Business School, 1980. From government data.
a. U.S. data.

Table 5.7
Advertising expenditures of manufacturing subsidiaries in the Philippines serving local market only

Industries' (three-digit SIC) expenditure on advertising as percentage of sales[a]	Investors[b] from other developing countries		Investors[b] from United States	
	Number of subsidiaries	%	Number of subsidiaries	%
Low (less than 1%)	7	87.5	45	71.4
Medium (from 1% but less than 2%)	0	0	2	3.2
High (2% or more)	1	12.5	16	25.4

Source: Vinod Busjeet, "Foreign Investors from Less Developed Countries," unpublished doctoral dissertation, Harvard Business School, 1980. From government data.
a. U.S. data.
b. Those serving the Philippines only.

Table 5.8
Advertising expenditures of manufacturing subsidiaries in all locations

Industries'[a] expenditure on advertising as percentage of sales[b]	Subsidiaries of developing country investors		Subsidiaries of United States investors[d]		Subsidiaries of other industrialized country investors	
	Number	%	Number	%	Number	%
Low (less than 1%)	785	84.2	6,196	73.8	4,926	80.1
Medium (from 1% but less than 2%)	122	13.1	1,183	14.1	728	11.8
High (2% or more)	25	2.7	1,020	12.1	496	8.1

a. Three-digit SIC level if corresponding advertising data available; otherwise, two-digit SIC level.
b. U.S. data.
c. Data bank for this study.
d. Data banks for Harvard Multinational Enterprise Project. U.S. data to 1975. Other industrialized country data to 1971.

that strategy has on occasion worked quite well in developing countries. For example, a U.S. multinational's dominance of the Tehran detergent market was challenged before the revolution by a local brand, with the unfortunate (to an English speaker) name of "Barf." The local manufacturer seems to have correctly concluded that Tehran held enough price-sensitive customers that a well-packaged, cut-price detergent would gain a certain popularity against the highly advertised products. In 1969, it sold for some 30 percent less than a leading U.S. brand, Tide.[14] It appears that the strategy paid off. In another case, while Union Carbide was offering locally made Eveready flashlight batteries in Indonesia for 55 rupiah, a Singapore-owned firm was producing and selling in Indonesia similar batteries, with little promotion, at 35 rupiah. Locally owned and Singapore-owned plants held substantial market shares through similar low price strategies for soft drinks and plastic sandals. The story has been repeated for many products in developing countries.[15]

In sum, the available data and the impressions from interviews suggest that most of the firms from developing countries have used price as their principal marketing weapon abroad. They have a tendency to invest in industries that are not generally characterized by large marketing expenditures; their not infrequent investments in other industries are usually associated with strategies that emphasize price rather than product differentiation.

One might wonder why, if price cutting is a reasonable option, multinationals from the industrialized countries do not themselves rely more on price and less on other marketing tools. Whatever the reasons, other studies have shown the relative inflexibility of U.S. firms with respect to price when they operate abroad.[16] For some multinationals, their reason is high production costs, of course. Inefficient at low volumes due to their large-scale, capital-intensive technologies and high overheads, certain multinationals find such a strategy to be unappealing. But costs are probably not prohibitive in some simple consumer goods. For such products, the competitive advantage that U.S. and similar firms have exploited has typically been in brand development. Once that advantage is abandoned, the firms may have no special skills and enable them to survive abroad.

To be sure, some of the price-oriented strategies followed by developing country investors are quite sophisticated and take into account the kinds of problems faced by a multinational from an industrialized country that would compete on price. A drug manufacturing firm grew out of a chain of pharmacies in one Southeast Asian country. When foreign exchange shortages made importing difficult in the years immediately after World War II, the group began to manufacture drugs from imported ingredients. Gradually, the enterprise developed more manufacturing capability and began to produce some of the ingredients that it had been importing. Managers soon learned that manufacturing costs of the drugs could be quite low. As one of the managers put it to me: "If an American manufacturer sells a capsule at 35¢, his manufacturing costs are around 5¢." Out of this awareness developed a clearly enunciated and successful strategy. The manager continued: "If the American firm can produce the capsule at 5¢, we can certainly manufacture it at a cost of no more than 7¢. If we sell it for 10¢, we have a good margin. Indeed, in our country 35¢ for a capsule is prohibitive for most customers. We need to spend very little on promotion if we can sell it at 10¢. Of course, we don't have much R&D to cover." When asked why the U.S. firms fail to sell in the Asian market at 10¢ to cover only their variable costs rather than surrendering the market, the answer was that they would run into trouble with the U.S. government. They had been severely attacked in the past in congressional inquiries for selling drugs to foreign customers for less than they charged American customers. The Asian manager continued by explaining how the firm acquired the technology:

We can copy most drugs quite easily, so the task is to handle the patent problem. Our government requires that patented products be manufactured locally for the patent to hold. Moreover, the government limits royalty payments to 5 percent of sales. Thus, early in the life of a new product, we approach the foreign manufacturer, show him our ability to manufacture the product, and ask for a license. He has little choice. He can try to manufacture locally himself, but he is not very attracted to the small market and realizes that we are likely to produce a substitute product and undercut him so much that his plant will be a failure. Usually we get the license.

When asked how his plant compared to that of an American pharmaceutical company, the manager said that the Asian company manufactured a very wide range of drugs but only in batch runs. The firm had fabricated many of its small tanks and other equipment itself. By 1977, the firm had exported its strategy to other Asian countries. Plants abroad were outfitted with equipment made in the investor's home country or reproduced locally according to the designs used at home.

In sum, most foreign investors from developing countries derive their competitive advantages from the technologies that enable them to manufacture at low cost. These technologies involve small-scale, flexible, labor-intensive plants and, frequently, considerable use of local inputs. For some firms, the advantages derive from innovations of products especially suited to the environments of developing countries. With relatively rare exceptions, most foreign investors from the developing countries exploit these advantages by charging low prices to attract customers away from alternative suppliers whose prices and costs are higher. Those competitors may spend large sums on advertising and other marketing efforts, such as trade names; foreign investors from the Third World usually do not.

6

Motivations for Foreign Investment

Many firms in developing countries have competitive advantages similar to those identified in this study but have not decided to invest abroad even though they might earn substantial returns by doing so. They have never considered the possibility, or they have thought the risks to be too great. Why did the developing country firms in this study decide to establish foreign subsidiaries?

Studies of enterprises from the industrialized countries have suggested that managers who do exploit a competitive advantage in foreign markets are likely to do so first by exporting products. Rather than scanning the world for the best ways to utilize its advantages, the firm is likely to take up opportunities that offer a satisfactory reward and that require the smallest number of changes in the company's established operations. Thus, managers are likely to prefer exporting over establishing a foreign subsidiary that can use the company's skills in a foreign market. Most firms from industrial countries begin foreign manufacture only when the continuation of exports is threatened.

The behavior of managers of firms from developing countries differs little from that of managers of enterprises from the industrialized world. Most firms identified in this study exported before they manufactured abroad and undertook foreign manufacture when threats appeared to their ability to hold foreign markets previously captured by exporting. But there were other motivations.

Defending Export Markets

There is considerable evidence to support the proposition, implied in chapter 2, that exports have been the first step to foreign investment for most firms in this study. The link between exports and investments is apparent for the firms identified in the data bank for this study, although data were available for only a few subsidiaries. Exports preceded the establishment of foreign subsidiaries in about 85 percent of the cases. The pattern is consistent with data available from other sources. Researchers have reported that a high percentage of parent enterprises in Latin America had previous experience abroad before establishing foreign manufacturing affiliates. Exports came before investments in 25 of the 30 cases examined.[1] The Latin American study not only linked experience in foreign markets to subsequent investments in those markets but points out the protected nature of most of the markets into which investment has flowed.[2] Barriers to trade were such that exports would not be a viable form of business for the long run.

Asian firms have behaved similarly to Latin American firms. In a study of 23 Southeast Asian firms, 19 had exported to a market before investing there.[3] Two UNCTAD reports provide additional support for the link between exports and investment.[4] For this research, various foreign investors from developing countries were asked why they invested abroad. Table 6.1 reports the responses of Indian managers, which were typical of the responses by managers from developing country firms. In small, medium-size, and large firms, threats to export markets provided the principal incentive for investing abroad. The results are similar to those in another study of Indian foreign investment.[5]

There are differences in motivation between developing country and advanced country firms, according to interviews with foreign investors in Thailand. The same questions were asked of both kinds of firms, allowing a direct comparison between the two groups. The results are shown in table 6.2. Foreign investors from developing countries place greater emphasis on diversification of risk than do their counterparts from advanced countries. The motivations that are of average importance to developing country investors are much less important to traditional multinationals that have gone to Thailand. Defense of export markets seems to be a major form of motivation for both types of investors.

Interviews in Mauritius and the Philippines with a small number of subsidiaries from developing countries serving the local market suggested behavior similar to that uncovered in Thailand (table 6.3). Frequent explicit statements underlined protection of markets as a very important motivation, but limits on expansion at home were also often mentioned, as in the Thai interviews. The emphasis on limited opportunities at home came primarily from enterprises from India, where antitrust actions have severely restricted domestic expansion. Limited growth opportunities at home played little role for investors from other

Table 6.1
Motivations for foreign investment by Indian firms

Motivations	Number of small firms (fixed assets of 1 to 50 million rupees)	Number of medium-size firms (fixed assets of 51 to 100 million rupees)	Number of large firms (fixed assets of 101 million rupees or more)	Total number of responses[a]
Protection of export market	21	10	7	38
Similar technological requirements in host country	19	6	6	31
Host country investment incentive	15	9	6	30
Expansion to new markets	10	4	5	19
Indian domestic growth restrictions	7	7	4	18
Cost advantages	13	3	1	17
Other	2	2	0	4

Source: Interviews conducted by Carlos Cordeiro.
a. Each of the 52 firms interviewed could answer to more than one kind of motivation.

countries, even though their home markets were usually smaller than the Indian market. In those countries, firms could expand at home by diversifying into other lines. Although antitrust legislation restricted Indian firms from diversifying further at home, restrictions on capacity expansion in India explicitly exempted capacity for export operations. Thus, Indian firms could, in theory, expand by exporting. If exports were to remain feasible, Indian firms could have grown by building capacity at home to supply foreign markets, but the ever-present threats to exports seem to make such a strategy unviable. Thus, even for the Indian firms, threats to export markets play a major role in their decisions to invest abroad.

The relationship between countries' trade patterns and their foreign investment positions provides evidence of a very different sort to link exports with foreign direct investment. For fifteen developing countries, data were available that showed their total stock of direct investment in other countries. For the same parent countries, figures were available for exports of manufactured goods to other developing countries, the

Table 6.2
Rating of motivations for foreign investment in Thailand by firms from advanced and developing countries

Motivation	Average of ratings[a] by firms from advanced countries	Average of ratings[a] by firms from other developing countries
Threats to existing markets	8	6
Diversification of risk	1	7
High local return	3	6
Investment of accumulated local funds	1	3
Exploit experience with high-technology production	8	1
Exploit experience with labor-intensive technology	1	5
Relatives or countrymen business associates in LDC	1	5
Export capital equipment	2	4
A source of cheap labor	3	1
To export to the developed world	2	1
Use marketing expertise	7	1
Small markets at home	2	6
Circumvent tariff and quotas in developed countries	1	2

Source: Donald Lecraw, "Choice of Technology in Low-Wage Countries," unpublished doctoral dissertation in business economics, Harvard University, 1976. Data from interviews.
a. Rating based on scale of 1 to 10, ranging from unimportant to very important.

Table 6.3
Motivations of parents from other developing countries for foreign investment in the
Philippines and Mauritius for manufacturing subsidiaries serving the local market

Motivations	Weighted ratings[a]
Limited home market growth	12
Government incentives	11
Protect host country market threatened by tariffs	11
Exploit labor-intensive technology	7
Low labor cost	4
Minimize political risk	4
Export machinery	4
Exploit knowledge of host market	4
Access to third country markets	3
Access to raw materials	2
Use products of affiliates	2
Careers for family members	0
Encouragement by customers	0
Quality of labor	0
Circumvent quotas	0

Source: Vinod Busjeet, "Foreign Investors from Less-Developed Countries," unpublished
doctoral dissertation, Harvard Business School, 1980. Data from interviews.
a. Reasons ranked first received 4 points; second, 3 points; third, 2 points; fourth or less,
1 point.

destination of almost all the investment. The parent countries were
ranked by their recent investment figures, and these rankings were
compared to the results of ranking the countries by their manufactured
exports to other developing countries. Exports were considered for 1963
to allow for a lag. Table 6.4 presents the results. The Spearman rank
correlation coefficient between exports to developing countries and
investments is a rather high .80.[6] When the ranking of countries by
total manufacturing output was compared with the ranking for foreign
direct investment, the Spearman rank correlation coefficient was a much
lower .48. And when total exports were used rather than exports to
other developing countries, the ranking was even less closely related
to investment patterns.

As checks on the relationship between trade and investment patterns,
various refinements were made in the calculations. For example, since
Korean and Philippine investment figures included a particularly large

Table 6.4
Rankings of fifteen developing countries, by export of manufactured goods and foreign direct investment

Country	Rank by 1963 export of manufactured goods to other LDCs[a]	Rank by direct foreign investment[b]
Singapore	1	2
India	2	4
Hong Kong	3	1
Mexico	4	10
Argentina	5	8
Philippines	6	3
Brazil	7	7
Korea	8	5
Chile	9	12
Venezuela	10	6
Colombia	11	9
Peru	12	13
Ecuador	13	11
Bolivia	14	14
Paraguay	15	15

a. Calculated from table 12 in "Annex: World Development Indicators," *World Development Report, 1979* (Washington, D.C.: The World Bank, 1979).
b. See table 1.2 for dollar figures. Data for these figures are from various sources, which can be found in the footnotes for table 1.2.

fraction of nonmanufacturing investment, the rankings were recalculated to reflect only manufacturing activities. Further, instead of published data on volume of foreign investments, data collected for this study were used. For these calculations, more countries could be compared, but only the number of investment projects rather than dollar sums could be compared with other variables. Such changes did not significantly affect the conclusion that a strong relationship exists between a country's past exports of manufactured goods to other developing countries and later direct investment abroad.

If investment follows exports, one would expect a change in the mix of industries in which investment takes place when export patterns shift. Indeed, a former government official in Hong Kong described the historical investment patterns of firms from Hong Kong in the way one would anticipate. In the late 1950s and early 1960s, he reported, Hong Kong investors went abroad to make products such as enamelware and umbrellas, the kinds of items that Hong Kong had been successfully exporting. Later, they started plants abroad for flashlights and hurricane lamps, reflecting the next round of Hong Kong exports. Textile plants followed, with more recent investments in electronics and more sophisticated products.

The growth of manufactured exports from the developing countries seems to be a major factor in explaining the growth of foreign investment. From 1963 to 1977, Korea, Taiwan, Brazil, and Hong Kong increased their manufactured exports by ten to twenty times. Not only have total manufactured exports from developing countries grown rapidly but a large fraction of exports from certain of those countries have gone to other developing nations. In 1960, over 40 percent of the exports of Singapore, Taiwan, and Hong Kong, for example, went to other developing countries. Recently, significant quantities of goods have been exported from Brazil and Korea to other developing countries, a sure indicator of future growth in foreign investment from those sites.

Quotas and the Offshore Manufacturers

The firms that have established subsidiaries abroad to supply their customers in the industrialized countries provide no exception to the patterns just described. Most such offshore operations of firms from developing countries were established when exports from the home country were threatened by quotas.

A large part of the foreign investments to supply the markets of industrialized countries originated when restrictions were placed on textile trade in the 1960s. "Voluntary" restrictions were in effect on cotton textile exports from Hong Kong to the United Kingdom starting in 1959; the United States restricted imports starting in 1961.[7] A significant impact on investments was the revision in 1961 of the agreement between Hong Kong and the United Kingdom. Under the changes, quotas were broken down into several categories. The resulting restrictions appear to have had a greater impact on the larger Hong Kong firms than on the smaller ones. The larger firms were, of course, exactly the ones with the resources to go abroad. Hong Kong textile manufacturers reacted to limits on their exports by setting up plants in other countries where exports were not yet subject to controls. Starting in 1963, Singapore was the initial recipient of investments. Exports from Singapore to the United States and United Kingdom were not restricted by quotas. Further, Singapore provided an attractive site, since its exports benefited from preferences given by the United Kingdom to goods manufactured in the Commonwealth. Soon, however, cotton textile exports from Singapore were limited (by agreement with the United Kingdom in 1965 and with the United States in 1966), and exporters looked elsewhere for production sites. In response to the new round of controls, investment from Hong Kong and Taiwan went first to Macao, Malaysia, and Thailand. Gradually, exports from each of these countries were subjected to controls by the major importers. Investors then went further afield. One site was Mauritius, which has actively and successfully courted Hong Kong firms with its fiscal incentives and preferential access to the European Common Market.[8] By 1979, Mauritius could count at least 15 export-oriented textile plants established by Hong Kong parents. Indian firms also located in Mauritius, citing its preferential access to the Common Market as a major reason for investing there.

Not all the investments in "quota hopping" have worked out well. Countries that did not face quotas at the time of investment have generally fallen under quota arrangements as their exports have grown. Many firms have suffered when their host governments had to change the rules on exports after they invested. Governments have had to allocate quotas to individual firms. On occasion, they have given preference to locally owned firms. Sri Lanka, for example, has announced that it would discriminate by the ownership of plants and by destination of exports. Accordingly, Hong Kong firms were not to expect a share of the country's textile quota for the EEC, although they were to be allowed a part of expected U.S. quotas.[9] In some cases, governments have imposed informal restrictions on foreign firms regardless of the stated rules. Moreover, several foreign firms, in Mauritius, for example, have had difficulty with the Common Market's rules of origin, as more value had to be added within the EEC or its associates for products to qualify for special treatment in Europe.

Textile firms were only the pioneers in the movement of exporting firms abroad. More recently, companies have set up foreign plants for other products in order to escape trade restrictions. Perhaps a unique case appeared during the U.S. participation in the Vietnam war. A Southeast Asian firm set up a subsidiary in Guam to supply U.S. forces in Vietnam with products bearing a "Made in U.S.A." label. This subsidiary eventually fell as a casualty of the withdrawal of U.S. troops from Vietnam, but there are more permanent ventures. A Korean firm has established an export base for canvas shoes in Taiwan. Two Korean firms were negotiating a joint venture in 1980 with the Sri Lankan state leather firm for a plant to export canvas shoes.[10] Koreans planned a textile mill for Ghana to ensure access to the European market.[11] Similarly, a Korean enterprise applied to Portuguese authorities for permission to build an electronics plant in Portugal for export.[12] No doubt similar investments will continue as long as firms in certain countries face quotas imposed by richer countries to deal with trade adjustment problems.

In a few cases, import restrictions in the advanced countries led firms to invest in the industrialized countries themselves. Unlike the firms that invest in other less developed countries in response to restrictions, the firms that invest in richer countries leave the core of the manufacturing process at home. The advantage of the firms that export from poor countries to rich ones—the low cost of labor—cannot, of course, be exploited through investment in a richer country. Thus, the firm with manufacturing operations in an industrialized country usually undertakes most steps of the manufacturing at home, drawing on the cheap labor or other competitive advantages available there, and completes the last stages of fabrication in the advanced country. Such investments seem to account for most of the 23 manufacturing subsidiaries that were identified in my sample as being in industrialized countries.

This type of enterprise is exemplified by a furniture manufacturer from Hong Kong that manufactures furniture parts at home. The manager interviewed reported that its plant there is larger than and at least as automated as the typical U.S. factory. In addition, it has four plants in the United States that do final assembly. For such firms, the possible gains from U.S. assembly are many. Easy to identify are tariff savings (parts of products are often taxed less heavily than assembled final products) and lower transportation costs (shipments of parts are less bulky and less easily damaged). The assembly operations in the United States have provided more: a base for observing the U.S. market. The managers from Hong Kong regularly attend furniture shows to remain alert to designs being manufactured by competitors.

Other kinds of trade restrictions have caused exporting firms to seek overseas sites. In a few cases, export platforms were established in third countries because the inputs required for goods of international quality could not be brought into the home country. Raymond's (Indian) garment venture in Mauritius was established at least partly because high-quality components, such as zippers, that were required by the firm to sell its garments in the European market, could not be obtained in India.[13] Similarly, Anil Wire, another Indian firm, attributed part of its motivation for a Malaysian operation to its need for imported copper not available in India. Without quality copper, the firm could not make products of adequate standard to hold export markets. In the absence of import restrictions at home, such firms would probably have continued to use their home plants to supply export markets. Thus, their foreign investments were in response to trade restrictions, but not to those of the usual type.

The Search for Lower Costs

Restrictions on trade are not the only threat to continued exports to the advanced countries. Like firms from the industrialized countries that have set up offshore plants to supply their markets, exporters from the developing countries have responded to exports from other suppliers in countries with lower costs by seeking lower wages than their home countries offered. About 40 percent of the offshore investment identified in this study were to countries with lower wages than those of the parent's country. Hong Kong firms went to Macao, Mauritius, the Philippines, and Thailand, where wages were lower. Even though labor savings could not have been a major drive when they went to Singapore in the early 1960s, lower costs seemed to have played a role in later years.[14] Evidence from a number of export-oriented subsidiaries in the Philippines (9) and Mauritius (25) suggests that labor costs have played an important role in the location of operations there. When asked to rank motivations for their investments, the managers placed low labor costs at the top, with freedom from quotas next (table 6.5). In the Philippines and Mauritius, Hong Kong firms seem to have been the most sensitive to wage rates. Ten out of twelve such firms, all established recently, emphasized the low wages. Hong Kong wage rates rose rapidly in the 1970s and by 1979 had reached some $10–12 per day for skilled sewing machine operators, from about $1.50 in 1960.[15] In the Philippines a similarly skilled operator might earn a little more than $2.00.

In some cases, managers reported shortages of labor at home as the reason for foreign investment. Thus, Taiwan Pineapple suggested that it went abroad because Taiwanese workers were simply not willing to work on pineapple plantations. Some Hong Kong firms also cited labor shortages at home as reasons for recent moves to Sri Lanka.[16] It is difficult to tell whether the shortages are really different from wage pressures, since one cannot determine whether more labor would be

Table 6.5
Motivations of parents from other developing countries for foreign investment in Mauritius and the Philippines for manufacturing subsidiaries serving export markets

Motivations	Weighted rating[a]
Low-cost labor	43
Avoid quotas	36
Government incentives	17
Encouragement by customers	15
Access to third country markets	12
Careers for family members	11
Use products made by affiliates	10
Exploit experience with labor-intensive technology	9
Minimize political risk	8
Quality of labor	5
Limited home market growth	0
Protect host country market threatened by tariffs	0
Export machinery	0
Exploit knowledge of host market	0
Access to raw materials	0
Pressure to earn foreign exchange	0

Source: Vinod Busjeet, "Foreign Investors from Less-Developed Countries," unpublished doctoral dissertation, Harvard Business School, 1980. Data from interviews.
a. Reasons ranked first received 4 points; second, 3 points; third, 2 points; fourth or less, 1 point.

forthcoming at home if the firms were to offer higher wages. But managers seem to view shortages of labor as something that cannot be solved by increases in pay that would leave them able to compete in international markets.

A few foreign investments have been made in third countries to save on transporting inputs to the production process. Thus, some Taiwanese plywood and veneer firms established Singapore factories to save on transportation for Malaysian logs.[17] By 1979, Korean plywood manufacturers were moving abroad for cheaper labor as well as to save on transportation costs for materials.[18] Without such low costs, they would probably be unable to hold on to their traditional customers. Again, foreign investment was motivated by a barrier to trade, but this time one not imposed by government.

The search for lower costs seems to be undertaken by managers, no matter what their origin, principally when competition makes the current cost level unacceptable.[19] Without competitive pressures, managers appear to remain in their original location. The possibility of larger profits from lower production costs elsewhere is not sufficient to induce most managers to incur the expenses of searching out foreign sites and deal with the risks of investing abroad. Like American firms, which typically establish offshore sources only when imports make U.S. costs uncompetitive, most developing country firms established their foreign export plants for defensive reasons: to build protection against the effects of quotas on their exports or to survive against aggressive competitors with lower costs.

Ethnic Ties

For a number of firms, ethnic ties have had a major influence on decisions to become involved in production in other countries. The extensive overseas communities of Chinese and Indian origin have served to encourage exports that have led to investments. Ethnic ties have also, in some cases, provided a direct link that generated investment without previous exports, even when specifically ethnic products were not involved.

Numerous studies have emphasized the role of information when a manager is considering an international business activity.[20] No matter whether the decision involves exports or foreign investment, a firm must somehow learn about the opportunities. The cost of acquiring reliable information about foreign markets is large, and it is likely to seem particularly burdensome for the relatively small firms from developing countries. If someone trusted by the manager is resident in the potential market, the cost of acquiring believable information is likely to be much lower than if the home firm has to send its own personnel abroad to study opportunities. Overseas Indian and Chinese communities provide exactly this kind of link for firms from India and for Chinese managers from Southeast Asian countries. In fact, in many cases, the initiative for business comes from overseas Indian and Chinese businessmen. With knowledge of the local market and access to a distribution system, they seek out suppliers whom they know and trust. For the overseas Indians, likely suppliers are Indian firms; for overseas Chinese, likely suppliers are in Hong Kong, Singapore, or Taiwan. In many cases, the contacts lead initially to export sales, which may, of course, be followed by investment. In other cases, international contacts between businessmen from the same ethnic community have led directly to investment. In these cases, the investing firm gains enough believable information to skip the export stage.

The importance of ethnic ties is illustrated in both Thai and Indian data. In Thailand, investors from other developing countries identified "relatives or countrymen-business associates" as playing an important role in their decisions.[21] Not surprisingly, the same factor played only a small role for the multinationals from advanced countries in Thailand. Interviews with firms in India indicated that Indians abroad were their most important source of contact for the initial investment (table 6.6). The importance of overseas Indians in making connections for foreign investment has also been pointed out in other research.[22]

The role of ethnic ties is evident in another way: in the partners chosen by foreign investors from developing countries. Interviews in the Philippines revealed that at least a part of the locally held equity in subsidiaries is owned by parties of the same ethnic group as the parent in nine of twelve cases. In six of them, the same ethnic group owns more than 90 percent of the local holdings. In Mauritius, ethnically related parties hold equity in eight of sixteen cases; in seven of the cases, related parties own more than 90 percent of the locally held shares.[23] The person providing the initial reliable information or establishing the first contact frequently turns out to be the business partner for both trade and investment.

One might expect Hong Kong, Taiwan, and Singapore investors to have local partners from the same ethnic group when they go to the rest of Southeast Asia. As expected, their partners are typically Chinese, but they are not necessarily from the same subgroup. The overseas Chinese business community in Singapore, Malaysia, Thailand, and Indonesia is made up largely of immigrants from southern China: Hokkiens, Hakkas, Cantonese, and Teochews, for example. While a large fraction of the Hong Kong Chinese are of Cantonese origins, a significant part of the business community in Hong Kong and Taiwan is not from southern China. The Hong Kong textile industry is dominated by Shanghai Chinese, for example. As a result, joint venture arrangements in Southeast Asia generally cross dialect lines.

It might come as a surprise that ethnic ties play a less important role in Latin America than in Asia. The common language and national origin of Spanish-speaking Latin Americans might lead to the easy flow of reliable market information across Latin American borders, but this does not seem to be the case. The resulting high cost of information about foreign markets may, like government policies, be an important

Table 6.6
Principal sources of foreign contact and information for Indian foreign investors

Host country	Number of investors with sources of contact and information						
	Export agent, distributor	Indian expatriate	Host country government	Indian bank	Foreign bank	Local (host country) individual	Other
Malaysia	4	5	5	4		1	4
Indonesia	2	3					
Singapore		1	1				
Philippines					1		
Thailand		1					
Hong Kong	1						1
Fiji		1					
Afghanistan		1					
Sri Lanka	1	1					
Nepal						1	
Dubai	2					2	
Iran	1						1
Iraq							
Qatar			1				
Mauritius		2			1	1	1
Nigeria	1						
Zambia	1						
Kenya		2					
Canada	1	2					
West Germany							
United Kingdom	1	1					
Total	15	20	7	4	2	5	7

Source: Interviews by Carlos Cordeiro.

Table 6.7
Foreign manufacturing subsidiaries of firms from developing countries

Sales of parent	Number of subsidiaries
Less than $5 million	26
At least $5 million but less than $50 million	27
At least $50 million but less than $100 million	21
At least $100 million but less than $500 million	42
$500 million or more	31

Source: Data bank from this study.

factor in explaining the smaller trade in manufactured goods in Latin America and hence the smaller flows of foreign investment.

Ethnic differences seem to have an impact not only in providing information that identifies foreign business opportunities but also in placing constraints on the ability of firms to manage scattered units of an enterprise. Most firms in this study were small, family owned, and family managed. Even though many firms held a large share of their home markets, the majority were small by international standards, with half of the parent firms reporting sales of under $100 million (table 6.7). Of the firms for which figures were available (parents of 90 subsidiaries), more than two-thirds had less than $50 million in assets. In eleven of seventeen small Indian companies (less than 10 million rupees), all the equity was held by one family. In five of the remaining six firms, more than half of the equity was held by a single family. Although many of the larger Indian "houses" have brought in professional management from outside the family, family ties are still important for many.[24] In large Chinese firms, such as Tatung, the founding family also still holds a great deal of power.

The role of family is important in the operation of foreign subsidiaries as well as in identifying opportunites for trade and foreign investment. Family firms frequently send family members abroad to represent their interests. This has been true even in early foreign investment from Latin American countries (S.I.A.M. di Tella, for example). At least for Chinese firms, and probably for others, posting relatives abroad simply extends the tradition of appointing kinfolk to authority at home when the owner is absent.[25]

Many researchers have pointed out the coherence and trust within the Chinese extended family.[26] The Chinese family-run business has a large number of reliable people to identify overseas opportunities, to hold management positions within the core enterprise, to manage subsidiary units located far from direct family control and supervision, and to establish other business ties. Many other cultures do not typically provide the family firm with similar opportunities.[27] In Latin America, the lack of trust within most extended families of Spanish origin and the difficulty of keeping family members in the business can impose a constraint on growth, particularly abroad, where regular monitoring of managers is difficult. A study of Mexican agrarian elite, in describing the nature of decision making in enterprises, suggests the difficulties that a far-flung business would face in a culture in which trust does not extend widely in the family: "Most such decision making is done at the level of the nuclear family where a man will sometimes discuss his possible strategies with his wife or with his most intimate compadres. With few exceptions, a farmer will not make critical decisions with his brothers or with his father."[28] One Mexican's description of the Mexican personality is similar:

Yes, we withdraw into ourselves, we deepen and aggravate our awareness of everything that separates or isolates or differentiates us. And we increase our solitude by refusing to seek out compatriots, perhaps because we fear we will see ourselves in them, perhaps because of a painful, defensive unwillingness to share intimate feelings.

Every time a Mexican confides in a friend or acquaintance, every time he opens himself up, it is an abdication.[29]

The difficulty of exchanging information, extending trust across a wide group of related people, and holding family members within an enterprise seems characteristic of all the Spanish community of Latin America.[30]

To be sure, many Latin American firms have grown large in spite of the usual limits that come from relying on a large number of family members. Nevertheless, the family structure imposes constraints on the ability of firms to obtain information from distant places and operate subsidiaries in places so far away that untrusted managers cannot be tightly controlled.

Even though the Spanish community in Latin America seems to offer little in the way of encouragement to trade and investment, ethnic factors do have some impact in the area. Ethnic ties influence Latin Americans of non-Spanish origins. Thus, Alpargatas, an Argentine firm managed by Argentinians of British origin, built up its association with its Brazilian affiliate through British and Anglo-Brazilian ties. Although the Brazilian affiliate has a history of more than 50 years, it, like its parent, is still managed largely by Anglo-Latin Americans. S.I.A.M. di Tella was founded by immigrant Italians in Argentina. By 1926, they had a close relationship with an Italian family in Chile. Eventually the Argentine firm developed a number of enterprises in Chile with the Italian Chileans.[31] Moreover, there are some firms owned by Latin Americans of Arab descent that have cross-border interests. On a very small scale, they reflect those of the Chinese and Indians in Asia.

In Asia, there is some evidence that the importance of ethnic factors declines as firms gain experience in particular countries. Although contacts through the Indian community were important for the first Indian ventures in Malaysia, those firms relied less on ethnic contacts in later years. However, such contacts continued to play a major role in Fiji, Hong Kong, and Sri Lanka, where the presence of Indian firms is smaller and more recent.

Diversification

On occasion, managers have sought out opportunities to diversify their holdings. The result is sometimes foreign direct investment, even though portfolio investment would, at first glance, seem to be satisfactory.

Many owner-managers in developing countries are concerned about political risk at home. Indian or Argentine managers, for instance, fear a left-wing government that will confiscate their properties. In such an environment, foreign investment provides a way of hedging. If the home country takes a turn for the worse, the firm's owners can leave and run the overseas subsidiaries. Thai data show that the drive by owners for diversification of risk is certainly a factor in leading developing country businesses to invest abroad (table 6.2). But the opportunities are limited, since, for investments that serve the local market, foreign firms cannot usually survive without some kind of special skill. For owners whose firms do not have advantages that can support direct foreign investment, portfolio investment is likely to be the route through which owners seek to diversify.[32]

Firms that serve export markets in the advanced countries have a special opportunity to diversify. They almost always have a competitive advantage—access to foreign markets—that can be transferred through direct investment to another developing country. Thus, an exporter eager for diversification finds some foreign investment a feasible alternative to investing all assets at home.

The drive for diversification seems to have been of considerable significance for the activities of Hong Kong and Taiwan investors. The special concerns of businessmen from those two island economies are quite easy to understand. Hong Kong will cease to be a viable capitalist economy if the New Territories revert to the People's Republic of China in 1997, when the British lease expires. The Macao incidents of 1966 and Hong Kong riots of 1967 served as a reminder of the possibility of takeover by China and seem to have stimulated investments abroad.[33] Taiwan stands ever under the threat of takeover by the People's Republic. In fact, the experience of the overseas Chinese throughout Southeast Asia teaches them that every site is potentially unsafe. Overseas Chinese have faced riots or worse in Indonesia and Malaysia and expulsion from Vietnam, for example. Confronted with uncertainties at home and the insecurity attached to any single overseas site, Hong Kong and Taiwan firms have a special reason for expanding their interests to a number of other countries. Direct investment, if feasible, would assure the refugee not only income but an honorable job.

Other Drives for Investment Abroad

Firms go abroad for reasons other than those already discussed. For a few projects identified in this study, the initiative for investment came from the government in a host country or from an international institution.[34] For example, the Kenyan government approached Birla of India for a paper mill. Birla was also approached by the International Finance Corporation when an American firm's (Spring Mills) textile subsidiary was in trouble in Indonesia. Packages Limited established the original contacts for its Zambian venture as a result of a suggestion by the International Finance Corporation, to which the eventual Zambian partner had turned for advice. In these cases, there was help in reducing the costs of learning about opportunites to profit from the firms' skills.

On occasion, finding jobs for relatives of owner-managers was one of the motivations for foreign investment.[35] In a number of developing countries, few good management jobs are likely to be available at home, since family firms, dominant in most developing countries, tend not only to be owned by family members but to be managed by them. Rarely are outsiders brought in to good jobs.

In at least one case, a firm from a developing country viewed its foreign subsidiaries as a training ground for its managers (in this case, not family members). The firm would select for foreign operations managers whose experience at home had been in a functional area, such as production. Overseas, they would be assigned to a general management position. If their performance at the end of the assignment was satisfactory, they would be placed in general management positions with one of the parent group's firms at home. Although the enterprise had not established foreign investments solely for the purpose of training, top management did view the training as a benefit to be added to the relatively low returns that the firm was earning from its overseas ventures. As the value of such training was being recognized, it was becoming a significant element in encouraging the firm to continue investing overseas.

In a few cases, manufacturing firms were pulled abroad by their home customer. Risks appeared minimal. As mentioned earlier, the Argentine firm of S.I.A.M. di Tella established its Brazilian plant when one of its major customers in Argentina, the British Shell Mex, asked the company to supply its Brazilian affiliate with pumps. A more complicated example is provided by two Indian cardboard manufacturers. In 1969, an Indian cardboard box manufacturer was approached by a group of Indian residents in Afghanistan who had heard that the country had been importing boxes from Sweden in order to package wine for export. In 1974, an Indian venture to produce boxes in Afghanistan was established in a pattern typical of those involving an overseas ethnic community. Meanwhile, the chief producer of raisins in Afghanistan, an American concern, was forced into purchasing boxes from this Indian-based venture because of the high tariff rate imposed by the government. According to the managing director of another Indian cardboard box manufacturer (the investing firm's main competitor in the Bombay area), he was invited by the American party to establish a similar operation in Afghanistan. This venture was, at the time of this study, still in the implementation stage.

There are some cases of investment abroad that seem to be quite special.[36] For example, a group of Malaysian owners of palm oil plantations banded together and approached an Indian manufacturer of soaps and refined oil about establishing a venture to refine edible oil and also produce a variety of soaps and other low-cost oil products in Malaysia. Apparently, since 1968, a lone Danish subsidiary had monopolized the processing of their oil. The Malaysian plantation owners were worried about their future because they were doing business in what amounted to a one-buyer market. In another case, an Indian textile company was involved in a management consulting contract with a textile mill in Bangkok. In 1974, because of domestic slack in demand, the mill found itself in a perilous situation. The Indian firm saw its opportunity and later that year acquired an equity share in exchange for new machinery and equipment. The strategy was one of expansion, and by 1977 approximately 50 percent of the mill's production was being directed at the export markets.

In sum, although the reasons for foreign investment have been varied, most firms have ventured abroad for defensive reasons, particularly when they could no longer serve foreign markets with exports. Close ethnic ties, contacts from customers, and the drive for diversification can also serve to overcome the managers' reluctance to put assets at risk overseas. Overall, most managers from developing countries appear to behave much like managers from the industrialized countries. The risks of foreign production are likely to be incurred only when there is no other way to hold onto a foreign market or when particularly reliable information makes those risks appear small.

Resulting Investment Patterns

The analysis of competitive advantages of previous chapters and the motivations for investment discussed in this chapter provide the material for explaining the investment patterns described in the first chapter.

First, the close relationship between exports and foreign investment explains, to a large extent, the differences in the number of foreign investors from different regions. Asian countries have led in the export of manufactured goods to other developing countries and also account for the largest number of foreign investors (666 manufacturing projects in the data bank). Latin American countries have lagged considerably in the export of manufactured goods to developing countries and have similarly lagged in foreign investment (157 manufacturing projects). Far behind both in manufactured exports and in foreign investment are the Middle East (with 68 manufacturing projects) and Black Africa (with 22 manufacturing projects).

The regional differences in export patterns seem not to be explained entirely by levels of development or other factors that might be thought to be related to exports of manufactured goods. The level of industrialization in the Middle East and Africa is probably too low for significant quantities of manufactured exports to originate there. However, Latin America's manufacturing sector is of a size comparable to Asia's.

Table 6.8
Number of foreign investments approved by Indian government in countries where Indians reside

Country	Indian population	Number of Indian investments
Aden	2,000	
Afghanistan	20,000	2
Australia	3,108	
Bahrain	5,500	
Burma	250,000	
Canada	52,000	2
Ethiopia	4,520	
Fiji	266,000	1
France	1,400	
Ghana	1,750	
Grenada	9,500	
Guyana	357,000	
Hong Kong	5,000	1
Indonesia	27,617	8
Iran	1,000	3
Iraq	12,000	1
Israel	23,000	
Jamaica	27,951	
Japan	1,141	
Kenya	139,593	2
Kuwait	12,006	
Laos	1,800	
Madagascar	12,350	
Malawi	11,299	
Malaysia	910,000	24
Mauritius	575,123	8
Muscat	4,500	
Netherlands	1,500	
New Zealand	6,700	
Nigeria	1,600	1
Philippines	2,516	4
Qatar	2,000	1
Rhodesia	10,000	
St. Vincent	3,703	
Saudi Arabia	1,035	
Singapore	150,000	5
Somalia	1,360	
South Africa	620,436	
Spain	1,600	
Sri Lanka	1,224,784	1
Sudan	2,550	
Surinam	101,715	
Tanzania	85,000	
Thailand	18,014	2
Trinidad	360,000	

Table 6.8 (Continued)

Trucial States	5,000	
Uganda	50,000	
United Kingdom	750,000	1
United States	32,000	
Vietnam (South)	2,000	
West Germany	4,681	1
Zaire	3,000	
Zambia	10,705	1
Other (Dubai, Nepal)	1–9,000	5

A recent study examined value added per capita, population density, and several other economic factors as indicators of export levels for Asian and Latin American countries.[37] After these factors were taken into account, there were still large differences between Asia and Latin America that could be explained only by characteristics of the regions. The poor performance of manufactured exports in Latin America, as compared to Asia, probably results largely from differences in government policies. The long-standing emphasis on "inward-looking" development strategies in Latin America has created high-cost manufacturers, which can compete only with great difficulty in export markets. Further, the emphasis on import substitution has led most Latin American countries to erect high barriers to imports of manufactured goods. As a result, many efficient firms have found neighboring markets to be closed to exports.

Second, most subsidiaries of firms from developing countries are located in countries with similar or lower levels of development than that of the parent countries because of the nature of firms' advantages. Small-scale technology, ability to use local inputs, and so on are advantages only in countries with markets similar to or smaller than those of the parents. Such skills are not advantages in richer countries.

Third, investments go, to a great extent, to neighboring countries because of the trade patterns. Exports generate investments if the exports are to countries to which the firm's advantage can be transferred. Exports to similar or poorer countries have been largely to countries in the parent's region. Thus, investments have been largely regional.

Finally, the ethnic role has had some influence on investment patterns. Indian firms, for example, have gone to Hong Kong and, even more, to East Africa. Significant numbers of Indians live in both places. Nevertheless, if countries are located far away from the home country, even the existence of an overseas ethnic community seems to play little role in attracting investment. Guyana and Trinidad, for example, have large Indian communities but have not attracted direct investment from India (table 6.8).

7   Invest or License?

Although previous chapters described the kinds of advantages that enabled certain firms from developing countries to survive abroad as foreign investors, they did not explain why the parent firm chose to establish its own foreign subsidiaries. When a firm intends to profit from the use of its competitive advantage overseas, it might choose to sell its skills or other advantages to an enterprise located in the foreign market. The sale would involve a license, a technical service agreement, some other form of contractual arrangement between the two firms, or simply the sale of machinery. Such arrangements would call for a payment by the enterprise acquiring the advantage in an amount that would take into account the return that the purchaser could earn from the use of the advantage. Such contractual arrangements represent a market approach to utilizing a competitive advantage. The firms in this study chose to establish a foreign branch or subsidiary so that the transfer of advantage was "internalized" within the firm. The decision was, in most cases, made for good reasons.

The choice between using the market or internalizing the transfer involves weighing, at least implicitly, a series of costs and benefits. If the transfer is made internally to the firm, the enterprise must reckon with certain problems that are faced by foreign-owned subsidiaries or branches. A foreign business is usually viewed by the host government as less desirable than a locally owned firm. Moreover, the foreign firm bears additional overhead and faces the consequences of probable mistakes from management's lack of intimate familiarity with the local environment. On the other hand, contractual approaches such as licenses pose different problems for the firm that has advantages to transfer internationally. Nevertheless, a great deal of technology and other know-how is transferred from developing country to developing country through market arrangements.[1] Thus, the Indian Oberoi hotel group has simple management contracts for several overseas hotels that bear the Oberoi name. Mexican and Brazilian firms have sold steel technology abroad without any equity investment. And manufacturers of machinery in Brazil, Argentina, India, Korea, Taiwan, and Singapore have transferred technology through simple sales of machinery. For developing country multinationals, however, the problems of using the market outweighed those of internalizing the transfer of advantages through direct investment. Still, the majority of the enterprises identified in this study chose to give other firms some role in the transfer.

Problems of Contract

The Need for Security

The advantages of many firms, whatever their national origins, are of an intangible sort. They consist of skills, know-how, reputation, or information. Unlike physical assets, intangible assets can be transferred to others without reducing the supply of the asset at home. Once others hold the assets, however, the new owners can use them in various ways or pass them on to still other enterprises.

Although conveying the advantages to others does not diminish the *amount* of skills, know-how, or information available to the originating enterprise, it may diminish their *value*. If a Hong Kong enterprise, say, sells its know-how to a firm in Indonesia, the acquiring firm can use it there and obtain whatever monopoly profits are associated with the advantage. These profits are thus lost to the originating firm, which presumably was appropriately compensated. If the Indonesian firm passes the knowledge on to a company in, say, Malaysia, the Hong Kong firm loses the opportunity to sell know-how to that Malaysian firm or to gain monopoly profits from using its competitive advantage in that market directly. In an extreme case, the Indonesian firm might use the know-how to manufacture in Indonesia and export products to Hong Kong, competing with the originator of the know-how and thus lowering the return to the Hong Kong firm from the use of its special skills in its own home market.

It is not only the Hong Kong firm that might encounter difficulties in such a transfer. The Indonesian firm that acquires the advantages faces certain risks as well. If the Hong Kong firm were to sell its skills to still another Indonesian company or to a company elsewhere that exports to Indonesia, the original Indonesian firm that purchased the skills would face competition and might earn less on its acquired advantages than it originally expected.

There are contractual arrangements designed to limit the risks undertaken by both the seller and the purchaser of such intangible assets. If the hypothetical Hong Kong seller provides the Indonesian firm with know-how under a licensing or technical assistance contract, the agreement might restrict the use of the knowledge to a certain geographical region. If the know-how can be patented, the Hong Kong firm can gain further protection by registering its patents in various countries not covered by the agreement. The Hong Kong seller could try to extract from the Indonesian firm the lion's share of the monopoly rent that the knowledge could earn in a specified region. Moreover, the contract might protect the Indonesian firm's purchase by prohibiting the Hong Kong firm from selling similar information to another firm that will operate in the buyer's geographical area.

In some cases, the problems of protecting the security of a firm's competitive advantage are apparent at the very outset of negotiations. In certain transactions, the potential buyer finds it very difficult to determine the value of the information without being privy to a significant part of the details about the information. The seller is, of course, reluctant to reveal much of the knowledge before negotiations are concluded. Especially if patent protection is not secure, revelation may enable the prospective purchaser to take advantage of the skills without payment. Again, some contractual arrangements are designed to deal with this problem. The potential buyer may sign a secrecy agreement at the outset, promising not to reveal or to use the information revealed to him until a mutually acceptable arrangement is worked out. There are, however, serious difficulties with such agreements.

The problems of security play another role when second-hand machinery is involved. A number of developing countries prohibit the import of used equipment or require special permits that are in fact rarely granted. Quite a few managers interviewed for this study admitted that their firms had repainted second-hand equipment and sent it as new machinery to subsidiaries in countries that restricted imports of used equipment. Keeping such a transaction secret is not easy if it involves unrelated parties.[2]

Although contractual solutions can be designed to cover most problems of security, in many cases they do not provide enough assurance to induce independent parties to undertake the transaction. The problems are especially severe when developing countries are involved.

The potential contracting parties have well-justified fears. Legal systems in many developing countries provide little protection in case of disputes. First, in some of the poorer countries, commercial law is underdeveloped. Second, in a wide range of developing countries the formal legal system is rarely relied on for business matters. Rather, disputes are settled according to local norms and among acquaintances. An outsider is unlikely to feel assured of fair treatment. Finally, parties to contracts fear that the costs of litigation in another country, even when that option is realistic, would be prohibitive.

The potential problems inherent in contract negotiation and enforcement can be avoided if the firm establishes its own affiliate abroad to make use of its competitive advantages. If technology is passed to a subsidiary, profits from the use of technology accrue to the parent whether the know-how is used to serve local or export markets.

Imbalance of Information

Even when security of information is not a problem, the firm that offers to sell a competitive advantage may have more information than the buying firm[3] or vice versa. Even if the firm with more information is willing to reveal it, the other party may not have confidence in the reliability of what it is told. For example, suppose the competitive advantage of a Hong Kong firm lies in the possession of appropriate machinery. A simple way of profiting from the machinery would be simply to sell it to an Indonesian firm. The Hong Kong firm might be quite willing to provide information about the machinery; however, the Indonesian buyer is likely to doubt the accuracy or completeness of the data received. If the equipment is newly manufactured by the Hong Kong firm, it is unlikely to have an established reputation. As a result, the Indonesian buyer will consider the purchase of Hong Kong machinery as entailing a risky decision. Only the Hong Kong firm knows how good the machinery is.

If the relevant machinery is second-hand, a potential indigenous buyer is also likely to be in a disadvantageous position. Even if the local firm knows about the availability of second-hand machinery, perhaps through dealers in such machinery, the risks associated with purchase seem to be high. The variance in performance of second-hand equipment is extremely large.[4] The purchaser needs access to some measures of the recent efficiency of the machinery, such as its output and maintenance records. Often these records are not available with the machine, or when they are, they are viewed with suspicion by a potential buyer. When dealers in second-hand equipment are involved, the risk may be reduced, but only somewhat. Most are generally distrusted by buyers.

As in other cases, some security is available from appropriately designed contracts. Agreements might obligate the supplying company to assist in installation, to provide training or personnel, and to guarantee the performance of the machinery. The contracts are, however, likely to be enforceable only with considerable difficulty and expense when developing countries and international boundaries are involved, for the reasons already mentioned.

If the problem of using the market for transferring competitive advantages lies in lack of information that is trusted by both parties, internalizing the transaction by establishing a subsidiary can eliminate the problem. When second-hand equipment is being transferred within the same enterprise, for example, experience with the equipment in one location allows a good estimation of its operating costs in a new location. Moreover, technicians familiar with the particular machines can be made available within the enterprise for installation and technical help. There usually are no problems of distrust between parties with different interests.

Even if a firm is not transferring the second-hand equipment from one of its own plants, it may still hold an advantage over a potential local competitor in obtaining such equipment. In many cases, the foreign firm has already established ties with dealers that enable it to locate and evaluate second-hand machinery. As a regular customer, the firm may receive more reliable data on the condition of the equipment, or at least it may have confidence in its ability to evaluate the information made available. An inexperienced potential buyer would not be likely to trust information from the experienced firm, and building up the same knowledge and relationship with suppliers is a time-consuming, expensive task.

The problems of contractual arrangements pointed out thus far can occur even when the relationship between the buyer and the seller of know-how might be of short duration. In such cases where the technological skill could be mastered rather easily by a buyer if the selling firm reveals the information or the technology could be transferred through the movement of machinery, the costs to the selling enterprise of transferring its advantages are likely to be fairly predictable at the outset. Many transactions, however, do not meet these criteria, and they raise still further problems.

Multiple and Uncertain Contingencies

When a long-term relationship between the firm with an advantage and its potential purchaser is inevitable, transactions involve uncertain costs on the part of the firm selling its advantage. Moreover, the buyer finds it difficult to specify clearly the performance standards to be met by the supplier of skills. In long-term agreements, the parties may have to make provisions to cover a wide range of contingencies, such as the possibility that know-how will be used to manufacture slightly different products in the future or that the production of the same products will require different technologies.

As an illustration of the kind of problems that arise in long-term contractual relationships, consider another hypothetical Hong Kong firm, this time a textile manufacturer with an advantage in its access to export markets in the advanced countries. The Hong Kong company's customers view the original Chinese firm as a reliable supplier. To make use of the company's tie to buyers, a firm providing goods under contract will need a long-term relationship with the Hong Kong company. For, say, a Mauritius firm to be provided with access to the Hong Kong firm's market in an industrialized country, the Hong Kong firm would agree to design the items to be manufactured, specify quality, and guarantee for the buyer the performance of the Mauritius plant. In turn, it would probably insist on the right to have inspectors in the Mauritius plant to monitor performance and demand heavy penalties should the Mauritius firm not meet schedules or quality standards, since failure there would harm the Hong Kong firm's reputation.

At the time of negotiation, the products to be manufactured over the next few months by the hypothetical Mauritius firm are likely to be known, but the parties are unlikely to know at that time exactly what will be produced and under what conditions manufacturing will be done over the next few years. New products or new quality standards for manufacturing, or new customers obtained by the Hong Kong firm, are all likely to involve changes in prices, commissions, delivery schedules, quality standards, and machinery. Further, the Hong Kong firm is likely to want special treatment given to certain orders, perhaps because particular customers generate profitable business for the Hong Kong parent. Such special arrangements are likely to be difficult to predict at the outset. As a result, contracts are unlikely to be adequate for business to be conducted, unless they are unrealistically complex.

The need for contracts that cover numerous contingencies can arise even in seemingly simple supply arrangements. An Indian firm explained that its investment in Europe resulted from the difficulties of arranging contracts to cover all the contingencies involved in selling dies to an independent party. Since the dies exported from India were, in many cases, not perfect, they had to be altered on arrival in Europe. Since the nature of alterations and corrections was difficult to predict and cover in a contract with an independent European company, the Indian firm established a subsidiary to handle the work.

Even the various kinds of contingencies that have been described thus far do not cover all the uncertainties. The arrangement between the hypothetical Hong Kong firm and the Mauritius firm may have a finite life, although neither party is likely to admit it when the original negotiations take place. With time, the Mauritius firm will establish its own reputation with buyers abroad. If other Mauritius firms begin to export, buyers from the advanced countries will visit Mauritius to make their own arrangements directly. Eventually, the Hong Kong firm will be viewed as decreasingly important to the success of the Mauritius company, and any fees paid to it will be viewed as an unnecessary and inappropriate burden. The relationship is likely to end. Although a contract might, in theory, take into account the finite life of the arrangement, such a contract is unlikely to be forthcoming when the parties find it difficult to confront the possibility at the time of negotiation.

The problems of contract are likely to be particularly great for foreign investors from developing countries, whatever markets they serve. The kinds of technology they transfer make the usual arrangement long term and, at the same time, difficult to predict. The transfer of the types of skill involved in small-scale manufacture is more difficult and, thus, more time-consuming than is the transfer of some of the technologies provided by many multinationals from the advanced countries. Lack of experience on the part of the supplying firm makes the exact time and costs difficult to forecast.

The particular problems of transfer for firms from developing countries are reflected in the training requirements. Training a manager for a factory that is labor-intensive and designed for maximum flexibility is quite different from training a manager for a more automated factory that mass-produces certain products using technology that is common to a large number of factories of the enterprise. The latter kind of manager can rely heavily on standard operating procedures and standard reporting systems, which can be provided in a package that includes manuals, drawings, or standard forms. The required work force includes many low-skilled or highly specialized laborers. The necessary training can be imparted rather quickly. In contrast, the manager of a small-scale, flexible plant must continually juggle people of broad skills. Rather than having primarily low-skilled workers, or highly specialized ones, he must assemble and manage a group of workers that can take on a range of tasks. He must adjust production schedules to match demands for various products. Further, his management tasks differ from day to day. Troubleshooting is an essential skill. While the manager with standard equipment from the advanced countries can rely on parts air shipped from his home country when his machines break down, on available repair manuals, and on standard engineering procedures when technical problems arise, the manager who has special machines and second-hand equipment must arrange for repairs of machinery for which parts often cannot be simply ordered from the machinery manufacturer and for which repair manuals and procedures are unlikely to be at hand. As a study by Peter Blau demonstrated, "As one moves from small-batch to mass production, the nature of manufacturing tasks becomes more uniform, which is reflected in an increase in routine work, a lower skill level of the labor force, and reduction in support components. And . . . mass production routinizes work and simplifies the administrative structure."[5]

The task of locating raw materials and components may also complicate the job of a manager of a small-scale plant. The manager using technology from an advanced country can predict his needs comparatively well and can often depend on affiliates in the multinational system to supply them. In contrast, the manager with a shifting product mix must buy varied inputs in small quantities. In many cases, he must obtain inputs locally. Although international sources involve long lead times and heavy cost penalties, the use of local materials involves constant searching and evaluation of scattered, often technologically weak, suppliers.

The problems faced by firms from developing countries when they transfer their kinds of technology show up in the subsidiaries' use of many more expatriate managers and technicians than are found in subsidiaries of multinationals from the industrialized countries. In the 30 subsidiaries in Mauritius and the Philippines for which data are

Table 7.1
Average number of expatriates in manufacturing subsidiaries in Mauritius Export
Processing Zone (1970–1978)

Home of investors	Number of observations	Average number of expatriates		
		After 1 year of operation	After 2 years of operation	After 3 years of operation
Developing countries	12	11.25	9.75	6.33
Industrialized countries	14	1.29	1.14	.79

Source: Vinod Busjeet, "Foreign Investors from Less-Developed Countries," unpublished
doctoral dissertation, Harvard Business School, 1980. Data from government data.

available, home country managers and supervisory technicians accounted for more than 90 percent of total personnel in those job categories in 14 subsidiaries; more than 60 percent in 24. And whether the subsidiary served the domestic or export market seemed to have no impact on the use of home personnel. For Mauritius, data were also available that permitted a comparison of firms from different home countries. Table 7.1 clearly points out the greater propensity of firms from developing countries to use expatriates in their subsidiaries. (The relationship holds if expatriates are counted as a percentage of the work force as well.)

In Indonesia, the differences between firms from developing countries and elsewhere are particularly noticeable. Table 7.2 shows the average number of expatriates in projects owned by investors of various nationalities. Only the Japanese come close to the expatriate employment of the subsidiaries of parents from other developing countries.

Details are available for a small number (22) of Indian joint ventures abroad. In only three of the projects were there no Indian managers; in at least 13 the managing director was Indian (table 7.3). Similarly, Indian technical personnel were almost invariably present in the subsidiaries. In only 1 case out of 23 was there no Indian technician (table 7.3).

Evidence of the greater role of expatriates in the subsidiaries of parents from developing countries comes from a sample of 23 such firms and 130 multinationals from the advanced countries, all operating in Southeast Asia. The ratio of foreign to local employees was also found to be higher in the developing country firms.[6]

Table 7.2
Number of expatriates in manufacturing subsidiaries in Indonesia (1967–1976)

Home of investor	Average number of expatriates per project
Chinese in Hong Kong, Singapore, and Taiwan	14.4
Other Southeast Asian countries	11.6
Other developing countries	20.0
Japan	11.1
United States	5.0
United Kingdom	5.6
Other industrialized countries	6.9

Source: Data for realized projects from Indonesian Investment Board.

Table 7.3
Number of Indian technicians and managers in foreign subsidiaries of Indian parents

Number of Indian technicians	Number of joint ventures
None	1
1–10	8
10–25	2
42	1
Unknown quantity	7
All technicians Indian	4

Number of Indian managers	Number of joint ventures
None	3
Only the managing director	7
Unknown quantity	6
All (including managing director) Indian	6

Source: Interviews conducted by Carlos Cordeiro.

The information from the data bank for this study shows the large number of expatriates active in the subsidiaries studied. The median number of expatriates per subsidiary was 14;[7] the average, 25. Of course, the large number reflects, to some extent, the fact that most of the subsidiaries were established in recent years, and skills were still being transferred. The figures for all the subsidiaries are, however, quite comparable to those for Indonesia, where investors of different nationalities were compared. No significant relationship existed between nationalities and ages of projects, and the use of expatriates was much greater in the developing country firms. Thus, one can fairly safely conclude that the data do show a higher propensity among firms from developing countries to use expatriates, and not simply because most of the subsidiaries of such firms are young.

I believe that the greater use of expatriates by developing country investors is a result primarily of the nature of the technology to be transferred. One could, however, argue that multinationals from the advanced countries have greater incentives than the firms from the developing countries to substitute local managers for expatriates, as expatriates from industrialized countries cost more.

There are, however, still other reasons why it takes firms from the developing countries longer to transfer technology than firms from the advanced countries. Many multinationals from industrialized markets have had previous experience in transferring know-how. Even at home, they have branch plants that have had to master skills developed in other parts of the enterprise. And the considerable turnover of personnel, particularly in U.S. firms, provides a need to develop a way of transferring skills from manager to manager. In addition, many firms from the advanced countries have had more experience abroad than the typical developing country investor. As a result of the experience at home and abroad, some have felt the need to develop standardized approaches to transfer. The experience has encouraged such firms to reduce a great deal of the know-how to manuals, drawings, or specifications and to standard operating procedures that describe scheduling, maintenance, and other operations. As a result, skills can be transferred more easily and quickly. Firms from developing countries have not had such experience.

In sum, both the nature of the technology transferred by foreign investors from developing countries and the lack of experience of most such enterprises make the period of transfer lengthy and the costs difficult to predict. Further, the nature of the technology and the lack of experience make it difficult to spell out standards of performance during the training period. As a result, a contractual arrangement has to cover an unusually wide range of contingencies.

Even when the time period is long and there are many uncertainties, a contract could, in theory, take into account all feasible contingencies, calling for a schedule of adjusted payments or other actions in response to each plausible future event. In reality, when the number of possible events that would affect the arrangements and the uncertainty surrounding costs and other matters is large, a contract is likely to be too complex to be negotiated.[8] If the transfer is made between a parent enterprise and its subsidiary, the difficulties are greatly reduced.

Rather than enter a complex contractual relationship or form a subsidiary, a firm has another option. It might decide to enter a short-term contract with another enterprise. The two parties could negotiate new arrangements in the future when events change. Since the legal systems in some developing countries are not adequate for enforcement of a formal, complex arrangement, this alternative is particularly appealing, at least in theory.

Such open-ended arrangements are feasible alternatives to long-term contracts or direct investment when both parties have other parties to which they can turn should new negotiations fail to provide satisfactory terms when events force changes in the business arrangements. Thus, a garment maker in Hong Kong does not require a long-term arrangement with a U.S. importer/distributor. The firm's sewing machines can be used to supply slightly different products to a large number of alternative buyers. Similarly, the U.S. buyer can invest in building a U.S. distribution system with confidence that other suppliers would be available should future negotiations with the Hong Kong firm break down. In a large number of cases, however, such alternative partners are not quickly or easily available. The investments involved in the first round of transactions are such that the costs of switching to other business partners are high.[9] Illustrative would be a U.S. company that assembles furniture for a Hong Kong firm that supplies parts. After the initial investments, the relationship takes on the characteristics of a "bilateral monopoly." Neither party can find a quick substitute for the other if they should fail to reach agreement on terms for, say, a replacement line of furniture. There are few firms in Hong Kong accustomed to producing quantities of standardized furniture parts for export. Thus, the assembler is unlikely to have a handy source of components exactly suited to its factory should the original agreement terminate. Moreover, there are few firms in the United States that assemble furniture from imported parts. And most of those that do exist are closely tied to an existing parts supplier that can satisfy their needs. As a result, the Hong Kong firm will fear that it will lose valuable sales in the U.S. market while it searches for a new firm willing to invest in a furniture assembly plant and obtain the needed market access should the terms of the old firm be unreasonable at some future date. The problems between independent parties are even more difficult, of course, if either party has to invest in special equipment that is useful primarily in the relationship with the other party. The manufacture of certain electronics components requires such specialized investment. In such an event, arrangements are particularly likely to be unsatisfactory.

In spite of the problems, within a single country open-ended arrangements are relatively common, even when the conditions approach that of a bilateral monopoly. In a few cases, government regulation assures the parties of a viable long-term relationship. In the United States an investor can build a pipeline to a gas field that is under different ownership. Although the gas field operator is dependent on the pipeline (and the pipeline owner, on the gas field operator), the government provides assurance of transport rates that are reasonable to both parties, even under unplanned future contingencies. Thus, both are willing to commit funds to their respective projects. For most international transactions, however, there is no equivalent regulation.

Open-ended arrangements exist for some domestic relationships even in the absence of government regulation. A manufacturer of automobile parts in the United States may be willing to invest in a plant even though the firm sells most of its output to a single automobile firm. For the automobile assembler, the one parts company might represent the major portion of its supply of the particular part. If a future year's automobile design calls for a much different version of the part, the two firms must negotiate a new arrangement. Although firms with such business ties usually attempt to diversify their customers or supply bases, such companies have accepted for many years the uncertainties associated with open-ended arrangements in bilateral monopoly situations.

A key to tolerance of open-ended arrangements, in the absence of government regulation, lies in the trust by parties that, when future negotiations are needed, neither will attempt to take full advantage of the other. The requisite trust is likely only when the two parties share a common business culture.

A high order of trust rarely exists when the parties to a potential agreement are of different nationalities and ethnic groups. Intimate knowledge of business norms is unusual when different cultures are involved, but without it neither party can leave important matters to be negotiated later unless there are other firms to pick up the relationship with little cost should negotiations fail.

Examples of trust across cultures do exist. International financial markets rely heavily on trust, but the number of important institutions is relatively small, transactions are so frequent that trust can be built up (and if trust is violated, the offender will be punished by exclusion from future transactions), and most transactions are completed in a relatively brief time span. Other examples of trust exist between non-banking firms from different developing countries as well. Chinese firms in various countries of Southeast Asia work out business arrangements that spell out little in the way of responses to contingencies. In fact, a number of joint ventures exist with no formal written contract whatsoever. Any problems will, it is assumed, be settled according to unstated norms accepted by both parties. Nevertheless, even within the overseas Chinese community of Southeast Asia, there is less trust than one might first expect. In many cases business arrangements cross intra-Chinese ethnic divisions. In these cases, there seems to be less trust than when only one Chinese group is involved. Even though the Chinese do not always trust each other, the greatest problems with open-ended contractual arrangements arise when the gap in business norms is larger. In the interviews for this research, Chinese businessmen frequently made comments about the untrustworthiness of Indonesian, Malay, and other Southeast Asian managers. Of course, Indonesians and Malays had similar comments about Chinese businessmen.

Contractual arrangements that depend on future negotiations provide solutions to problems of multiple or difficult-to-predict contingencies only under very special conditions. For many firms that face long-term ties, it would seem better not to sell competitive advantages at all. For them, the establishment of a subsidiary to exploit the advantage internally is an attractive solution to the problems of contract.

The Issue of Image

Although matters of security, imbalance of information, and the handling of future contingencies are the most pressing problems of contractual arrangements, they are not the only matters that make investments preferable to market mechanisms for many firms to profit abroad from their advantages. On occasion, an important element of image seemed to be associated with ownership.

Firms from developing countries were only infrequently led to investments by the need to emphasize brand loyalty and product images. The principal cases were the firms that manufactured ethnic products abroad. Just like the American customer who is suspicious that Danish beer bottled under license in the United States is not the same as what the parent firm produces, in spite of assurances to the contrary, an overseas Chinese or Indian might be suspicious of noodles or gripe water made under license by a local firm. And might not even an Englishman expect more authentic Indian food in a London restaurant owned by a firm from India and run by its Indian representatives? No matter how faithfully products are reproduced abroad, in some cases ownership of the plant by the originating firm provides reassurance to the customer that is worth the costs associated with foreign investment.

Attaining Nonfinancial Goals

Even when contractual arrangements might provide perfectly satisfactory financial returns on the use of a firm's advantages abroad, some enterprises have other objectives that are not so easily served by contracts. The investors that want to find jobs for relatives of the owner-managers or that want to train employees from the home plant in overseas operations have particular difficulties with contracts.

In theory, contractual relationships with foreign enterprises could provide training for managers on rotation as well as jobs for underemployed relatives. In fact, the goals are not attained so easily with contracts. In making manpower decisions for a subsidiary, the parent can pay attention to the balance between return from training and the profits of the subsidiary. On the other hand, under a contractual arrangement the foreign party would probably insist that its profits be the principal consideration in job assignments.[10] When underemployed relatives are at issue, managers are unlikely to want to bring the issue openly to the negotiating table.

Closely related to the employment goal are the motivations underlying investments made to diversify the risks of a firm's owners. If financial diversification were the sole goal, the owners could accomplish their objectives through portfolio investments; there would be no need to establish controlled affiliates. But the objectives of diversification can be more complex. Some owner-managers want the assurance of a job should they have to leave their home country. This kind of security is easily associated with an overseas entity owned directly or indirectly by the home firm.[11] Similar security is not easily forthcoming from conventional contractual arrangements. Although one could, as in earlier cases, envision contracts to cover the eventuality that jobs might be provided by the licensee to managers of the licensor if political events were to drive them abroad, appropriate compensation might be difficult to arrange for such an uncertain event. Further, most owners would probably prefer not to face the issue so explicitly and are not likely to be confident that the contract will be honored if the feared political events occur. Direct investment comes much closer to providing the desired assurances.

Successful Contractors

At the beginning of the chapter it was pointed out that much technology is transferred without direct investment. The examples that were mentioned were all cases for which the problems of contract were not overwhelming. Oberoi, the Indian hotel group, faces no serious problem with respect to know-how. The hotel group's major asset is its name. Trade name legislation protects the name from theft. In fact, if the laws are inadequate, a potential user could steal the name regardless of Oberoi's business arrangments. Moreover, there is no serious difficulty with imbalance of information between the contracting parties. Although the relationship between Oberoi and a firm overseas is likely to be a long one, the contingencies to be handled in a contractual relationship are few and simple. For a hotel, the products and technology, for example, will undergo little change. Further, Oberoi's experience should provide it with a reasonable basis for estimating the costs it will incur in transferring its management know-how.

The transfer of Mexican and Brazilian steelmaking know-how illustrates the possibilities of transferring manufacturing technology without direct investment. Most important in the Mexican case is probably the fact that the Mexican oxygen reduction process has received so much international publicity that a foreign buyer is likely to have little question of the value of the process. Thus, there is not a large problem with imbalance of information between potential partners. The Brazilian case makes another major point. Although Brazilian processes have received less publicity than the Mexican process, other reasons make the market an attractive mechanism for transferring the know-how. One is the fact that Usiminas, one of the Brazilian firms involved in foreign sales of know-how, has had considerable experience in transferring its technology to Brazilian steelmakers at home. As a result, it should be able to estimate transfer costs reasonably accurately. More important, Usiminas is state-owned.[12] For most state-owned firms, foreign direct investment poses major political problems. Even if business reasons suggest that direct investment is the preferred alternative, the difficulties of explaining the use of public money overseas seem to push state-owned firms to alternative arrangements. In fact, very few state-owned firms with foreign manufacturing investments were identified in this study (a total of 66 subsidiaries).

In most cases, when technology is transferred through market mechanisms it appears to be of a widely available type. In these transfers, there are no significant monopoly returns associated with the know-how. In some such transfers, the mechanism is simply engineering consulting. The transfer is completed rather quickly, and few complications are likely to arise. For many other transfers with little proprietary knowledge, the vehicle is the sale of turnkey plants. A large part of the technology is embodied in the machinery, although the supplying firm may provide technical help for the start-up. Again, there are no security problems, transfer costs are predictable, and the arrangement is so short term that there need be few provisions for future contingencies. Transfer of technology, in these cases, consists largely of the export of capital goods. The advantage of the supplying country usually lies not principally in innovations but in the fact that it is a low-cost producer of particular equipment, which might also be available elsewhere.[13]

Partial Internalization

Most of the firms that transferred know-how through direct investment have not completely internalized the transfer of their competitive advantages. They have chosen to involve a local firm to some extent in the transfer through a joint venture arrangement. Moreover, whatever the extent of ownership, most parents have not tightly controlled their subsidiaries. The willingness to involve local partners and the reasons for the considerable autonomy given to subsidiaries derive from the strategy of the firms and from the kinds of skills that they transfer.

Ownership

The frequency with which investors from developing countries involve local partners in their foreign subsidiaries is striking. Of the 602 manufacturing subsidiaries in this study for which data on ownership were available, only 57 were wholly owned by the parent enterprise.[14] Reports from other sources are similar.[15] This pattern stands in marked contrast to the ownership figures of U.S.-based multinationals. In 1966, nearly 60 percent of the manufacturing subsidiaries of American parents were wholly owned.[16]

The fraction of equity that foreign investors hold in their subsidiaries is a result of two factors: the desires of the investors, and the power investors can muster to impose their wishes on governments if the investors' desires conflict with those of their hosts. The desires of investors result from their ability to tolerate local interests and their need for the resources that local investors can provide.[17]

The ability of developing country investors to live with local partners is a function of the strategies such firms follow. Conflicts are most likely in enterprises that follow strategies that can easily pit the interests of the subsidiary against the interests of the rest of the enterprise. For example, if international reputation of brands is critical, a local partner who wishes to sacrifice quality to meet local demands is likely to be confronted by foreign owners who resist because of what lower quality might imply about their reputation elsewhere. Similarly, the firm that specializes production in subsidiaries of various nationalities and transships parts or various models among its affiliates is unlikely to be able to live with local partners. Allocation of orders, establishment of transfer prices, and expansion of production are likely to be viewed differently by the parent and a local partner who profits only from the operations of a single subsidiary. These were not the strategies usually encountered in the firms from the developing countries. Since the strategies of most investors from developing countries are unlikely to lead to conflicts between maximization in the subsidiary and the interests of the enterprise as a whole, joint venture partners' interests are unlikely to diverge greatly.

In unusual cases, developing country investors do follow integrated strategies, as has been pointed out. Not surprisingly, the ownership patterns of such firms are different from those of other enterprises from the developing countries. Consider the export-oriented investors, those which have chosen to serve their foreign markets from another base.

Almost 30 percent of the subsidiaries of those firms were wholly owned by the foreign parent. A study that contrasted the ownership of Hong Kong and Taiwan projects in Singapore found that Hong Kong firms are more likely to establish export-oriented subsidiaries and more frequently have wholly owned subsidiaries.[18]

Two Indian firms had wholly owned subsidiaries. One was a construction company established in Iran for the completion of a single contract. The other, a textile plant, was located in Mauritius to supply the Indian parent with materials; thus, a large degree of control was essential. The textile plant was established before the Indian government allowed the importation of textile machinery, and it was sold in 1972 after imports were liberalized.[19] In two other cases, Indian parents own more than 90 percent of the shares. One is a German manufacturer acquired for its facilities to service Indian exports. The second was a plant in Canada to distill and blend Indian rum. In these two cases, control was important to strategy and ownership was large in spite of the Indian government's position that Indian investors abroad should hold minority positions.

Korean foreign investments include an unusually large percentage of wholly owned subsidiaries: 161 of 243. However, 134 of the 161 wholly owned subsidiaries are for trading, and close links to parents would be expected. Most of the others are for real estate, construction, or raw materials. In manufacturing, only 2 of the 19 Korean subsidiaries are wholly owned by the Korean parents.[20] Thus, when manufacturing is involved, Korean firms appear to share ownership as frequently as the other foreign investors from developing countries.

There are no hard data about the benefits that the usual foreign investor from a developing country might expect from a local partner, but a study of U.S. firms provides grist for intelligent speculation.[21] U.S. multinationals that spent little on advertising found local partners valuable for their access to the market. Small firms also appreciated the capital and management that local investors provided. Firms from developing countries, usually small and typically without well-known trade names, would probably value highly the same contributions of local partners. The value of the benefits, whatever they are, seems to outweigh the costs for the vast majority of the firms in this study.

Host governments, of course, are likely to have little impact on the ownership policies of firms that prefer joint ventures. Those firms from developing countries that might see little benefit in local ownership

Table 7.4
Ownership of foreign manufacturing firms in Thailand (1962–1974)

Home of investor	Percentage of foreign ownership			
	100%	99.9–50.1%	50%	49.9–0%
Japan	25%	51%	10%	14%
United States	10	47	15	28
Europe	23	45	12	20
Developing countries	2	7	5	86

Sources: Donald Lecraw, "Choice of Technology in Low-Wage Countries," unpublished doctoral dissertation in business economics, Harvard University, 1976. Original data from Thai Investment Board and interviews.

probably cannot induce governments, in many cases, to allow their complete ownership, as their bargaining power is usually not great.[22]

The strategies of offshore investors leave little tolerance for a major voice by local partners. Their access to export markets eliminates the need for local partners who can make marketing contributions. And they are in a better bargaining position vis-à-vis the host government than are firms that will sell in the local market.

To ensure that the differences in ownership between firms in this study and investors from the United States and other advanced countries were not the result of a different mix of host countries, the ownership patterns for various investors were compared for several individual countries. These comparisons confirmed the differences between the ownership patterns of foreign investors from developing countries and those from industrialized countries, but they also suggested somewhat more complex patterns. Table 7.4, which reports ownership for several groups of investors in Thailand, is typical of the general results. As expected, investors from developing countries have wholly owned or majority-owned subsidiaries less frequently than do investors from advanced countries. On the other hand, data from some other developing countries show less differences than one might expect. In Indonesia, for example, parents from other developing countries own, on the average, 28 percent of the equity in their subsidiaries; other parents own only slightly more, 31 percent.

The small differences in ownership patterns in some countries are the result of the different behavior of large and small investors from the advanced countries. Small firms from the advanced countries appear to have ownership patterns similar to those of investors from developing countries. This should not be surprising, given the relationship between strategy and ownership. Small multinationals, regardless of their national origin, tend to follow strategies that do not require control over their affiliates. Moreover, they are likely to need assets when they invest abroad. Consequently, they find that the benefits of a partner with assets outweigh the accompanying sacrifice of some degree of control.[23]

The U.S.-based firms in Indonesia that were identified as "multinationals" (firms on *Fortune*'s list of 500 largest firms with manufacturing subsidiaries in six or more foreign countries), on the other hand, held, on average, 78.7 percent of the equity in their Indonesian projects. This figure is more than twice that for all firms from industrialized countries (and much higher than all U.S. firms). It is more than three times the equity held by parents from other developing countries.

Although the ownership patterns for firms from developing countries are quite unlike those of multinationals from the industrialized countries, the attitudes and behavior of the two kinds of firms appear to be quite similar. When a firm's strategy leads to potential conflict with local partners because of the interdependence of affiliates, joint ventures are less frequent whatever the firm's nationality. When each subsidiary operates to a great extent on its own, joint ventures can be tolerated and, in fact, are sought for the assets local partners can provide: money, management, knowledge of the local environment, or political influence. As a result, firms with strategies compatible with joint ventures only partially internalize their international business transactions.

Although firms from developing countries appear to be motivated in ways similar to multinationals from advanced countries when they decide on ownership policies, they may be more constrained by their home governments than are their multinational competitors. Tight foreign exchange positions at home cause governments to attempt to limit the ownership of their investors in foreign subsidiaries. India, for example, has insisted that most of its firms hold only a minority interest in overseas operations. Other governments have had a similar impact simply by limiting the export of foreign exchange for subsidiaries. Nevertheless, the data collected for this study suggest that home restrictions have not had a great impact on the degree of internalization. The ownership held in foreign manufacturing investments by parents based in Hong Kong, Mexico, and Singapore, which have few restrictions, is hardly different from that of Indian, Taiwan, Korean, Brazilian, Peruvian, and Argentine parents. Even after controlling for different strategies by considering only those subsidiaries manufacturing for the local market, almost exactly the same fraction of firms from the two groups own minority positions in their overseas operations. Indeed, although the numbers are very small for both groups, somewhat fewer subsidiaries of parents from restrictive countries are wholly owned by the foreign parent. On the whole, however, the needs of the firms lead them to seek local partners whatever their governments say.

Autonomy

Consistent with the willingness of firms from developing countries to share ownership in their foreign affiliates, a great deal of autonomy is typically granted to the managers of developing country subsidiaries. Apparently this autonomy is greater than that usually given to the subsidiaries of multinationals from industrialized countries.

The nature of the tasks to be undertaken influences the autonomy that is allowed to a subsidiary manager. The study by Blau concluded that "the more highly mechanized production is, the more likely it is that the final authority for making key production and marketing decisions rests above the plant manager's level than at his level or below."[24] Given the earlier description of the management tasks associated with mechanized production, Blau's finding should not be surprising. It suggests that subsidiary managers would have less autonomy in the typical firm from the advanced country than in the subsidiary of a firm from a developing country.

There are other reasons for the traditional multinationals to vest authority at a level higher than the subsidiary manager, reasons that are largely the same as those that push such firms to insist on a large amount of ownership in their overseas operations. Most managers consider ownership and control to be closely related. When results in one subsidiary are greatly influenced by the actions of another, decisions can rarely be left to the local manager's discretion. Thus, a multinational's strategy of relying on marketing techniques to differentiate its products requires, in many cases, close ties to the parent through ownership and control. Lower quality or other departures from standard in one subsidiary may ruin the brand image of the firm's products elsewhere in the system. Moreover, the technology implied by a particular strategy may influence centralization in ways other than that described by Blau. The large-scale technology used in the subsidiary may force its integration into the system. With large-scale technology, in some cases the only way even acceptable costs can be obtained is by some kind of integration across borders. The solution is likely to involve steps that increase interdependence among subsidiaries. For example, certain parts for which scale is particularly important are likely to be imported for a long time. Or certain components might be exported to other affiliates to make use of capacity. The resulting interdependence is likely to favor complete ownership and control from the center. Some multinationals from advanced countries might retain tight control because of their dependency on continued new inputs of technology to subsidiaries. In sum, there are several reasons why the subsidiary of the advanced country firm is likely to have a close relationship with other parts of the multinational enterprise. The close relationship is likely to entail external control over many decisions.

In contrast, the typical subsidiary of the developing country firm appears to stand alone. With the exception of the exporting firms, operations are usually not integrated with those of affiliates. Each affiliate tends to produce or buy locally for most of its needs, and only rarely does a subsidiary rely on its parent for a continual inflow of new technology or marketing techniques.

There is some rather hard evidence to support the claim that subsidiaries of investors from developing countries do have considerable autonomy. The managers of 30 subsidiaries in Mauritius and the Philippines indicated where certain kinds of decisions were made. Regardless of the market served, 24 indicated that capital expenditure decisions were made at home, but decisions about operating expenses and personnel policy were almost invariably made at the local level. For the firms serving the domestic market, decisions about prices and sale of products were always made locally. Even decisions about purchases and prices for inputs were not controlled by headquarters for the firms selling in the local market. Two subsidiaries indicated no parent involvement; 5 claimed joint decision making. Similarly, most decisions involved the subsidiary level in a sample of Indian firms that were producing primarily for the market of their host country.[25]

Firms from developing countries gave less autonomy to their foreign subsidiaries that manufactured for export. For the export subsidiaries in Mauritius and the Philippines, decisions about prices and sale of products were usually made at headquarters. Similarly, decisions about purchase and prices for inputs were generally controlled from home. Another study claimed a high degree of centralized decision making for exporting subsidiaries of Hong Kong and Taiwan parents in Singapore.[26] For these enterprises, performance in the subsidiary could have a major impact on the business of the parent or on opportunities for other offshore subsidiaries. Late delivery, poor quality, or other problems in the subsidiary could have a negative impact on the sales of affiliates elsewhere in these special cases.

To be sure, the allocation by most firms of a wide range of decisions to the subsidiary does not mean that decisions are made by nationals of the host country. The large number of expatriates in the subsidiaries certainly suggests a strong foreign influence. Nevertheless, the autonomy of subsidiaries and the frequency with which parents from developing countries share ownership with local partners suggest that decisions made at the subsidiary level are likely to be consistent with the interests of the local owners of the subsidiary. Local partners benefit only from the profits of the subsidiary, not from profits generated elsewhere in the international firm. Partners are unlikely to be silent with regard to decisions that adversely affect their financial interests.

Conclusions

The concepts of internalization, only recently applied to the issues of international investment flows, are as helpful in a study of foreign investors from developing countries as they have proved to be in studies of multinationals from industrialized nations. In general, when problems of security are great, when the same information is not available to potential parties to a contractual relationship, and when a relationship is likely to involve many and uncertain contingencies, both developing country and advanced country enterprises are unlikely to grant an independent firm abroad the right to exploit its competitive advantage but rather will invest in their own subsidiaries.

There are, nevertheless, some differences between firms from the developing countries and multinationals from industrialized nations that decide to transfer their skills. First, firms from developing countries are more likely to transfer skills to other developing countries, where the problems of contract enforcement are especially great. Second, in many cases the transfer involves a longer and more unpredictable relationship between supplier and user. Finally, nonfinancial goals may well be important to more of the firms from developing countries. The home countries of these firms are more likely to seem politically unsafe. And the family ownership of such firms enables nonfinancial objectives, such as employment of family members, to be passed from owners to the firms.

Firms from developing countries and those from the advanced countries also have different priorities for internalizing international transfers. For the latter, for example, the need to protect secret know-how may play a much greater role. In the absence of data for either group of firms on the total amount of know-how transferred through contracts, a direct comparison of these priorities remains elusive.

The data on ownership, however, do allow comparisons of the extent of internalization for those firms that do undertake foreign direct investment. Firms from the developing countries are more likely to take in local partners than are firms from the richer countries. But the factors that explain their ownership decisions appear to be quite similar to those that have proved useful in understanding the ownership decisions of multinationals from Europe and the United States.

8   Nonmanufacturing Investments

The focus of this study has been on the manufacturing investments of firms from the developing countries. However, the search for those projects turned up a number of overseas investments in services and in raw materials. In fact, some of the oldest projects and some of the most extensive international networks built by firms from developing countries are outside manufacturing. To present some observations about these activities is something of a digression from the mainstream of the book, but in some cases, the concepts that explain the non-manufacturing investments are similar to those that are useful for understanding manufacturing activities. In other cases, there are important differences.

The Service Sector

Financial Institutions

Perhaps the first overseas investment activities of many developing countries were undertaken by financial institutions. Already in the nineteenth century, Indians had a network of closely related financial activities throughout South and Southeast Asia. Perhaps not foreign investors in the strict sense of the term, the bankers in the network shifted funds from one country to another and internalized a large number of transactions that would have been more tedious if they had had to be undertaken among unaffiliated parties. The bankers had come from Chettinad, Tamil Nadu, and spread into Burma, Malaya, Thailand, Indonesia, and Mauritius. They were linked through an organization called Nattakottai Chettyar Association, which attempted to determine financial policies, fix credit terms, and assure liquidity of members.[1]

The affiliations in this early Indian network of some 1,500 banks enabled financial transactions to be made between parties who trusted each other, even though they were located in different countries. The need for trust has also played a major role in the establishment of the international financial institutions that have emerged more recently from the developing countries.

The total number of overseas affiliates of banks from the developing countries today is difficult to estimate. A U.S. Department of Commerce study reports 38 banks in the United States controlled by 24 parents in countries outside western Europe, Canada, and Japan. Most of these were from developing countries. They accounted for only some 7 percent of foreign banking assets in the United States.[2] In the literature search and interviews for this study, I identified 31 U.S. banks with parents from developing countries. Presumably, these were all included in the aggregate data from the Department of Commerce. For the whole world, I identified 341 foreign banks owned by a total of 61 parent banks located in developing countries.[3] Although no systematic effort was made to discover banks' foreign operations, the similarity between U.S. official data and information collected for this study suggests that the overall number identified might be a reasonable indicator of the total number of foreign banks.

The reason for the internationalization of banks is wrapped up in the principal role of a banking institution: to provide links among parties to a financial transaction. Among its many tasks, the bank stands as an intermediary that guarantees the pledges of parties to transactions; it matches maturities of obligations and takes the risk when no match is made; and it provides information to its clients, at least partially in exchange for the use of their funds. When transactions are international, the parties about whom information is sought or whose financial commitments are to be guaranteed are particularly unlikely to be known by the party seeking the bank's services.

As international trade becomes important to companies, their managers turn to financial institutions that can provide the special services they require.[4] Such managers place increasing demands on banks for quick responses about a wide range of conditions in various markets and about potential customers or suppliers. When international deals are struck, banks will be called on for letters of credit or other guarantees for transactions. As a result, when a bank's customers are engaged in international business, the bank risks losing them to competing banks if it is not able to obtain and transfer information across borders and provide other services.

In theory, at least, a bank need not establish branches or subsidiaries abroad to provide the required services. The bank does not have to know the foreign parties itself. Instead, it can trust an overseas bank to provide the information or guarantees needed for international transactions. In fact, there is a long history of "correspondent" relationships that are designed to provide exactly the kinds of links that banks need when they do not have foreign branches or subsidiaries. Thus, an Argentine bank can call on its New York correspondent for information about a prospective buyer of Argentine wheat; and it can call on the same bank to provide the letter of credit should the proposed transaction proceed. The Argentine bank would, of course, pay a fee for the services of its correspondent.

In practice, many banks have found such services inadequate. The managers we interviewed suggest that the fees are high and that when the volume of transactions is large enough, the bank can save money by establishing its own branch to handle the transactions. The customary rates seem not to take adequately into account the volume of business provided by the contractor. Why lower fees cannot be negotiated is unclear.

My own guess is that the fees are not really the critical issue. More important than cost is the speed and quality of service rendered. In practice, a bank has little ability to control the position of its requests in the queue of orders to be served by its correspondent banks; and it cannot easily make fine adjustments in the quality of service rendered. If an order is for a favored customer of the home bank, very quick service and thorough research may be important. The proper handling of the business matter, although the transaction itself may be minor, could be crucial for the retention of the customer's other business. When part of the returns from proper handling of the transaction accrue to the home bank from other business provided by the customer, it is difficult, as a practical matter, to rely on a correspondent bank for important services.

To be sure, like the international transactions of the exporting firms dealt with in earlier chapters, such banking problems could, in theory, be handled through complex contracts that call for the home bank to specify priorities and quality of service and pay fees according to varying scales. Or terms that specify speed and quality of service and the fees for various possibilities could be left open to future negotiations as the occasions arise. But for many manufacturing firms, neither the contingency contract nor the open-ended arrangements prove attractive. On one hand, the complexity required of the contracts becomes overwhelming if they are to take into account a wide range of possibilities, many of which are difficult to imagine in detail at the outset.[5] On the other hand, the option of leaving the contracts open to future negotiations is also not appealing. As would be the case for many manufacturing firms, the parties to a contract become dependent on each other. If future negotiations for renewal and for different services fail, the parties are likely to bear significant costs in searching out alternative partners; basic matters must be negotiated from scratch, new communications systems must be established, and so on. The fact that banks in different countries are more likely than manufacturing firms to share similar business norms and recognize these similarities could make it easier for banks to negotiate at a later date arrangements for future transactions. The nature of the transactions between banks, however, weighs in on the other side. Compared to manufacturing firms, banks are likely to be engaged in a large number of relatively small transactions. The costs of negotiating each on an ad hoc basis appear prohibitive, especially when the banks are separated by large geographical distances.

As a result of all these problems, correspondent relationships seem to survive only until a bank's business in a foreign market reaches a size that justifies investment. Eventually the correspondent relationship, based on standard fees for standard services, is likely to be superseded by the establishment of a branch or subsidiary. The allocation of charges then becomes a matter for internal management control and evaluation, not a matter of allocation of profits among the separate enterprises, each with a competing interest in the income. With transactions internalized within the enterprise, the bank can vary its service in different parts of the enterprise to reflect the benefits to the enterprise as a whole.

The distribution of overseas affiliates of banks from developing countries generally reflects the home countries' trade flows. In major export markets, banks are likely to have branches or subsidiaries to provide the services required for national exporters. Thus, Thai banks have established branches or representative offices in countries that provide major markets for Thai rice exports: Indonesia, Hong Kong, Singapore, and Japan, for example. Similarly, Bank Negara Indonesia has a Hong Kong branch with the primary role of financing the important trade flows between the two countries. (Very similar drives seem to have forced at least one accounting firm to spread outside its developing country home.[6])

U.S. banks have had an additional reason to go abroad: to provide a full range of banking services to U.S. multinational enterprises. Banks that could finance both parent and subsidiaries, transfer funds easily, and provide information about potential investment sites have had an advantage in holding the accounts of multinationals. But foreign investors from developing countries have probably not yet become sufficiently important to push banks from those countries abroad. Nevertheless, managers did point out the use by a Hong Kong bank of its Singapore branch to finance Hong Kong firms that were investing in Indonesia. And the Bangkok Bank Ltd. tells of its advantages of being multinational by drawing on the experience of a multinational customer.[7] It may not be long before investment as well as trade drives banks from developing countries to establish foreign affiliates.

The trigger that induces a bank to establish an affiliate abroad can come from the competition offered by the branch of a bank from an advanced country or from a local bank. Once a domestic bank faces a competitor that can provide good international services, the domestic bank may have to offer similar quality services to its local customers with international businesses or risk losing their accounts to the bank that can provide services.

Although international competition may be an important factor in inducing banks from developing countries to go abroad, there is some evidence that severe and long established competition can have the opposite effect. Thus, the Hong Kong Chinese, in spite of their extensive overseas investment and trading activities, have developed only a few banking operations abroad. One study reports a Hong Kong bank in Singapore, one in Malaysia, two in Thailand, with most operations in the United States (9) and Britain (3). In fact, most of the international spread of Chinese banks in Asia appears to be between Singapore and Malaysia. These banks probably became "international" only with the separation of Singapore and Malaysia, where they had established what had been "domestic" branches.[8]

The reason for the small number of international banks of Chinese origin may lie in the early spread of British banks in Asia. The Hong Kong-Shanghai Bank has long had affiliates throughout Southeast Asia and in London and New York. Its operations in Thailand have existed since 1888. Thus, this bank had served many of the international needs of the overseas Chinese communities throughout Southeast Asia for many decades before Chinese banks had the resources to establish similar networks.[9] Its long experience has, one would expect, generated economies that a new bank would find difficult to match. In recent times, Citibank and other U.S. banks have established operations in Hong Kong and the rest of East and Southeast Asia. Although they have provided a less extensive branch system than the British-run banks, they have also been able to serve the international business needs of the area. Financial services seem to be provided so extensively by the Hong Kong banks of British origin and by other multinationals that there is little room for the Chinese to enter. It may be too late for Chinese banks to launch a successful attempt to capture a large share of this business without a huge investment to overcome the barriers created by experience in the existing international banking networks.

Similarly in other parts of South and Southeast Asia European banks had an early start. The Chartered Bank of India, Australia, and China entered Thailand in 1894; the Banque de l'Indochine, in 1897. But in some countries, nationalizations and independence have weakened the hold of the European banks, leaving room for the spread of local banks. In a number of cases, the gaps created by the retreat of European banks have been filled by the international moves of banks from developing countries.

Banks' establishment of overseas affiliates differs in one significant way from the pattern that characterizes most manufacturing firms. Parents did not necessarily possess any particular technology or other know-how that gave them advantages over banks in their host countries. Overseas ties were usually a necessary extension for remaining competitive at home. Foreign affiliates did not have to stand alone in most cases. They were not in competition with banks in their host countries but provided services to the parent bank.

In other respects the internationalization of banks is quite similar to that of manufacturing firms. For many banks, once foreign transactions reach a certain volume, the disadvantages of contractual arrangements are outweighed by the advantages associated with undertaking the international transactions within the same firm. Further, like manufacturing firms, banks are particularly sensitive to threats. Although no systematic data were collected, it appears that the trigger for most banks to establish foreign affiliates is the fear that another bank will take away the firm's customers at home by providing better international services.

To be sure, not all overseas banking investments have followed the same patterns. On occasion, American banks have ventured abroad to exploit their retail banking skills. They have also sought foreign locations to obtain offshore deposits and attempted to diversify into activities closed to them at home by government regulation.

From time to time, a financial institution from a developing country also seems to have gone abroad to exploit certain skills. Bancom, a Philippine financial house with U.S. ties, spread to Hong Kong and other Southeast Asian countries primarily to provide money market and investment banking services. Although Bancom appears to have relied on certain competitive advantages, I encountered no banks from developing countries that went abroad primarily for retail business. However, a number conduct substantial business with expatriates from their home country who reside in the countries where they have branches. Thus, Pakistanis in New York are said to use regularly the Habib Bank for personal accounts and for remissions to family at home. One could argue that their advantage is the possession of a "brand name" familiar to ethnic Pakistanis located in other countries. Governments might view the encouragement of foreign exchange remissions as justifying the establishment of overseas branches (Habib is state-owned).

The major money centers, particularly London and New York, have provided an additional lure for banks from developing countries, usually those with dollar and sterling assets to manage. To be sure, a physical presence in the principal money markets for those assets is not essential for placing investments. The money could be managed at a distance, especially with the rapid communication now available. But even rapid communication of large amounts of data is not adequate to capture quickly enough the kind of information that is passed from person to person in the major financial centers. A personal presence in the market is viewed by many bankers as essential if funds are going to be handled well. Thus, a large number of banks from developing countries have located branches or other offices in New York and London.

Middle Eastern banks provide another exception to the usual pattern. Eighty foreign branches and subsidiaries of Middle East banks are recorded in the data bank for this study. This large number is hardly surprising, given their need to place in major financial centers large sums of money arising from petroleum sales. This spread is probably a result of the drive to be in major money markets rather than just the need to service trade or investment.

Hotels

In most cases, the strength of an international hotel chain is its name, no matter what the national origin of the enterprise. If travelers (or their travel agents) are familiar with the quality that is associated with a particular hotel name, they feel secure in booking a room from a distance without inspecting the hotel. Thus, the American businessman or tourist can reduce uncertainty by booking a Hilton, an Interconti-nental, or a Hyatt room when traveling to a country with which he is unfamiliar. The advantage of a known name is supplemented by a reservation system. If the traveler is staying in, say, a Hilton in one country, he can easily book a room in the Hilton of his next stopover; booking another hotel might be inconvenient for the traveler.

The advantages of the Hilton, Intercontinental, or other western names have a limited life with some travelers. If a traveler repeatedly visits the same city, he may discover local hotels of the quality desired. Or if colleagues have visited the city frequently, he may learn of local hotels even before his first visit. Thus, the international chains probably have their strongest advantage in cities that are relatively new on the business or tourist circuit and with first-time visitors.

Once familiar to the international traveler, a hotel based in a de-veloping country has an opportunity to take advantage of its reputation and expand abroad. As one might expect, hotel chains typically emanate from the more frequently visited sites among the developing countries. Since travelers from the hotel company's home country rarely provide a major market abroad, the hotels must depend on their reputations among travelers from the richer countries who have stayed at the parent hotel. Thus, one finds the Hong Kong Mandarin with a new "Mandarin" in Jakarta, and the Hong Kong Peninsular with a "Peninsular" in Manila. After all, a large number of businessmen who visit Indonesia or the Philippines have made frequent visits to Hong Kong. As a result, they would almost certainly be familiar with the Mandarin and the Peninsular hotels.

Although an established reputation gives such hotels a competitive edge over unknown local firms in foreign markets, their advantage over hotels from the advanced countries may be a bit tenuous. The "technology" of hotel management is likely to be rather similar, since the operations for the major international chains have virtually been reduced to manuals. The procedures can be mastered by hotels from developing countries, but probably not improved upon greatly. At least one of the hotel chains based in developing countries (Oberoi of India) was once affiliated with a chain from an advanced country and probably acquired much of its know-how through its old tie. To the extent that hotels based in developing countries do have an advantage over hotels from industrialized countries, at least part of it lies in the lower costs of management. To be sure, technology may undergo some adaptation as well. Accustomed to lower wage rates at home, managers of certain hotels in developing countries have created more personal service approaches in their practices than have the chains from countries with higher wage rates. Thus, a visitor to the Peninsular in Hong Kong discovers an abundance of "room boys" on each floor. On arrival, the guest is greeted with a cup of hot tea and perhaps a greeting from a room boy who has already learned the arrival's name. These services can be provided in other developing countries, where wage rates are also low. And they no doubt have an appeal to the international traveler.

Perhaps the largest hotel chain based in the developing countries is the Oberoi group from India.[10] Its operations are located in Egypt, Indonesia, Sri Lanka, Nepal, Tahiti, and Zanzibar. Some of the affiliated hotels involve direct investment; as of 1976, the Indian government reported five overseas hotels with Indian equity. Five more with equity were under construction.[11]

As has been mentioned, Oberoi sometimes invests; at other times, it simply sells its name with some management help. Like the hotels from the advanced countries, hotels from the developing countries have found that direct investment is not always necessary to their international spread.

In sum, the hotel chains based in developing countries seem to add to the unusual cases of international activities that draw their advantages from brand names. They fit with the bottlers and brewers. Moreover, the need for investing abroad to make use of the name does not seem to be overwhelming. The same firm may use a franchise in one case and direct investment in another. The choice probably has more to do with availability of funds by the parent and by a potential local partner than with the need for internalization. Although no attempt was made to determine what triggers led the hotel firms to go abroad, it is unlikely that the motivations were defensive, as has been so common for other investors. The nature of the product precludes exports as a first step that leads to commitment to foreign markets, and it is hard to imagine that business at home would be severely threatened by failure to go abroad.

Engineering and Construction

Engineering consulting firms from India, Brazil, and elsewhere have managed to build a very successful record abroad. In quite a few cases, they have established subsidiaries to handle their foreign projects. None was interviewed in connection with this study, but information from other sources suggests that some carry certain kinds of special skills when they go abroad and others do not.

It is possible that the provision of international engineering services, in many cases, represents little more than a trade in the factors of production. For example, in India engineers are in abundant supply. Rather than immigrating on their own to where their services are more in demand than at home, engineers have the option of associating with an Indian consulting firm that provides services abroad at lower costs than the services available from the industrialized countries. The firm provides an important service to the engineer. On one hand, many unemployed engineers cannot make the investment in seeking a position in another country. On the other hand, a firm from another developing country is unlikely to be fully trusted by the engineer were it to recruit directly in India.

Some engineers from India or other developing countries have something special to offer beyond their low wages. Their experience has taught them how to solve problems that are special to environments similar to those at home. Design of small-scale plants is such a specialty. Substitution of local materials may be another. Design of simple buildings suitable for tropical climates and low incomes is still another. A determination of the relative importance of these factors must await research on the consulting firms themselves, but the construction firms, about which more has been written, provide some hints that are probably applicable to both kinds of companies.

From Korea, the Philippines, Egypt, and elsewhere, construction firms have been successful in obtaining overseas contracts. In many cases, the jobs are accompanied with a permanent presence in the form of a subsidiary. Some indication of the importance of the activities of contractors from the developing countries is provided by published data. South Korean firms held $10 billion of contracts in the Middle East in mid-1980.[12] This reflected a steady growth from a total for overseas contracts on the order of $120 million in 1973.[13] Contracts in Middle East countries amounted to $6 billion in 1977[14] and $8 billion in 1979.[15] Indian firms reported $2.5 billion of foreign construction contracts no of January 31, 1980.[16] Of that, about 85 percent was in Iraq, Kuwait, Saudi Arabia, and the United Arab Emirates. At least 13 Brazilian construction firms had large contracts abroad in 1978. One, Constructora Mendes Júnior, had projects in Uruguay, Colombia, Bolivia, Algeria, and Mauritania. Another, Catento, was involved in constructing the Caracas subway and a railroad in Nigeria.[17]

In the Middle East and in Nigeria, the primary factor in the success of contractors from other developing countries appears to be their access to factors of production—construction labor and engineering talent—that are cheaper than those available at the construction site. Korean and Philippine firms bring whole crews to the Persian Gulf to undertake port and building construction. Korean firms had more than 61,000 Korean workers in the Middle East in 1973–1979.[18] Even Nigeria, short of skilled workers, has recruited engineers in Brazil.[19] In the Middle East oil-rich countries, little labor is available for construction work, and labor from the advanced countries would be much more expensive than even local labor. Nevertheless, like the engineers moved by the consulting firms, construction workers find it difficult to secure positions abroad without an intervening international firm. In fact, governments in some developing countries have required bonds of foreign recruiters because of their bad records of mistreating employees and not providing them with fares to return home. But countries such as the Philippines and Korea have organized labor markets that can provide the required skills at low costs to local entrepreneurs. Some with experience in construction work (in some cases for the U.S. military) have seized on the opportunities.

There is some evidence, however, that access to low-cost labor is not the only advantage offered by contracting firms from developing countries. The experience of such firms in working to developing country standards may provide an advantage as well, at least against competitors from the rich countries. The Mexican contractor that worked on the subway in Mexico City would, it seems, have most of the technical skills of a contractor with similar experience from the United States. Any missing skills are likely to involve the use of sophisticated machinery that substitutes for labor, skills not required where labor is relatively inexpensive. Moreover, the less expensive Mexican or other Latin American managers and engineers would be able to communicate with a Spanish-speaking (or perhaps Portuguese-speaking) work force. In addition, they would have skills in managing the kind of labor one finds in a developing country.

In an interview, the president of the Brazilian construction company Constructora Mendes Júnior stated that the company was most successful abroad with contracts for which they had had similar experience, such as "building roads and railways over very rough terrain." The firm claims to have gained a special advantage through its experience in operating self-sufficient work camps in isolated places and in working with an unskilled work force.[20] The company's abilities to hire low-cost employees, nevertheless, seems to have played a role in its success. For a road in Mauritania, the company brought along 400 Brazilian engineers.

Even firms from rich countries with backward regions claim advantages over other competitors from industrialized nations. A report on Italian construction and engineering companies attributes part of their success to their technical skills. Building conditions in developing countries are more like those of Italy, especially Italy's underdeveloped south, than those of the richer countries, and the Italian firms supposedly get along better with local workers and are more ready to train them, having had experience with peasants from southern Italy.[21]

The benefits a construction firm obtains from experience not only affect how it undertakes the job but enable it to estimate costs more accurately. The inexperienced firm is likely to build into its bid price a large margin to cover uncertainty. A firm from an advanced country may also bid high to cover the uncertainty of a strange environment and to cover the high cost of its personnel. The firm from another developing country with experience on similar projects is likely to offer the lowest bid, since it has fewer uncertainties than other competitors and cheaper resources than the firm from an advanced country.

Engineering and construction activities need not generate overseas investments, since services can be provided without a permanent foreign base. Nevertheless, some contractors have established offices abroad. An office may grow into a full-fledged operating subsidiary, or a firm may take an equity interest in the project it is designing or constructing.[22] The investment in a project would not typically involve management control, but there seems to be no regular pattern of investment.

Regardless of whether they establish subsidiaries, contracting firms are likely to have a particular incentive to seek jobs abroad.[23] The highly cyclical nature of the construction business in most countries should lead a firm to try to operate in several markets whose ups and downs are not synchronized. The established firm might well bid low for projects abroad when its own home market is depressed. The incentives to seek projects in other markets when business is slack at home are similar for contractors in developing countries and in richer countries.

In sum, the overseas activities of engineering and construction firms reflect something of a mix of trade and investment patterns. To a large extent, the activities are nothing more than the export of low-cost engineering and construction labor from countries where the labor is abundant to countries where it is scarce. But the firms also carry with them certain advantages in the form of skills, similar to those of the investors for manufacturing, derived from conditions of the home market. A firm from a country with excess workers is likely to be better able than a foreign firm to transfer the workers abroad. International contractual arrangements between workers and firms fail for reasons similar to those that explain the failure of contracts for many manufacturing firms. The triggers for overseas activities come, to some extent, from the cyclical nature of the home market, a factor that played little role for the manufacturing firms. The nature of the service, however, means that little direct investment is involved. Generally, the sum is no more than that needed to establish a sales office and, possibly, some management for projects.

Raw Materials

Some firms from developing countries have gone abroad to establish reliable sources of raw material for their home countries. In most cases, their motives have been similar to those of firms from the United States and Europe, such as the steel firms that have sought ores or other materials overseas.

The investments are from several countries and for a number of products. Hong Kong furniture manufacturers have established timber operations in Indonesia. An early Korean foreign investment (in 1963) was undertaken in Malaysia to secure timber for the Korean plywood industry.[24] In fact, by the end of 1978 about a quarter of Korea's overseas investments were for sources of natural resources.[25] These included numerous mining operations, timbering concessions, and fishing projects throughout the world.[26] The investment of one Taiwan firm was not in "raw material" of the usual vegetable or mineral type but a manufactured chemical. Formosa Plastics established a joint venture in the United States with ARCO (Atlantic Richfield Company) for polyvinylchloride, vinylchloride monomer, and ethyl dichloride. The goal was to obtain inexpensive plastics from the cheap ethylene available in the United States.

Raw material ventures account for a large fraction of the overseas investments of state-owned enterprises from developing countries. Iran, for example, attempted to secure sources of iron ore for two planned steel plants. The government steel enterprise put up money for the development of the Kudremukh iron ore projects in India in return for concentrates, prepared to specification for its gas-fired plants. Although a large sum of money (over $250 million) had been invested, the Iranian revolution put a brake on the cooperative effort.[27]

Several state-owned oil companies from developing countries have gone abroad to search for oil. A subsidiary of the Oil and Natural Gas Commission from India has participated in concessions in Iran, and Petrobras (through Braspetro, its international arm) from Brazil has negotiated exploration arrangements in other countries in Latin America, Africa, and the Middle East.[28] YPF of Argentina has participated in ventures in Bolivia, Ecuador, and Uruguay. The Chinese Petroleum Corporation of Taiwan has signed a contract for oil exploration in Colombia.[29] Most such ventures have been undertaken, it seems, by state-owned firms that were eager to capture a secure, inexpensive supply of oil for the nation. When a critical resource is involved, state firms appear able to overcome the political problems of investing abroad.[30]

Firms can obtain supplies of raw materials without direct foreign investment. In fact, a wide range of raw materials are routinely purchased on the open market. Thus, U.S. coffee processors acquire coffee beans from unaffiliated growers and feel no need to own coffee plantations overseas. Although there has been talk of foreign investment from OPEC countries in search of secure suppliers of food, nothing seems to have come of it.[31] The diversity of food sources seems, on the surface, to alleviate the need for direct investment. In most cases, the market provides a perfectly adequate solution to the materials problem if there are many suppliers and many buyers.

When suppliers are few, the purchasing firm might insist on long-term contracts before it invests in processing or distribution facilities. When purchasers are few, the supplying firm might insist on long-term contracts before it undertakes investment in a mine or plantation. In fact, for many raw materials such contracts can be quite simple in comparison to the kinds of hypothetical contracts that might govern manufacturing. The materials are, in many cases, easy enough to describe, since there are recognized standards for quality. The few contingency provisions are likely to focus on volume.

In spite of their simplicity, such contracts appear to be unsatisfactory in certain cases when international borders are crossed. For many raw materials arrangements, the costs of a breakdown in the relationship between supplier and user are likely to be particularly high. A steel plant, for example, may be designed for a particular type and grade of ore or pellets, and the concentrator or pelletizer at the raw material end may be built to serve the needs of a particular kind of plant. At the same time, enforcement of raw materials contracts may be particularly difficult in developing countries. Unlike the cases of hotels, government intervention against the foreign firm has been frequent for raw materials. Even the Australian government has forced the renegotiation of contracts between private iron ore mines in Australia and the steel firms of Japan.[32] Thus, contracts seem, in many cases, to provide little security. These problems are especially difficult when they are in addition to the usual problems that result from a firm's lack of trust in foreign legal systems or business norms.

When state-owned companies are parties, direct investment in raw materials may be undertaken for additional reasons. Security of supply may be an important national concern, but the risks may seem too high (or the profits too low) for a private firm to undertake the desired investment. The state enterprise may then undertake the investment, or, alternatively, the home government might provide incentives for its private companies to develop foreign sources of raw materials. Korea has followed both approaches.

The interviews for this study suggested that an occasional state-owned firm undertakes foreign investment for raw materials for still another reason. Managers of the Argentine national oil company, YPF, suggested that involvement abroad would enable it to work with foreign firms that have more advanced technology, which could be used to search for oil at home.

When multinational firms from the consuming countries appear to have tight control over downstream processing, as in aluminum smelting, state firms in countries that produce raw materials have attempted to increase their bargaining power by replicating the vertical structure of the existing multinationals. The result has been various plans for joint aluminum smelters, such as by Jamaica, Venezuela, and Mexico. By 1981, none of the proposed ventures had been established. In oil, however, projects have come to fruition. The National Iranian Oil Company took an ownership interest in an Indian refinery and a fertilizer plant and obtained a captive market through participation in a refinery in South Africa. By 1974, these refineries accounted for some 60,000 barrels per day of sales. In 1975, the Iranian company began negotiations to participate in a refinery in Senegal, and before the Iranian revolution, negotiations had even begun for joint refinery and distribution operations with ENI, the Italian state oil company.[33] In fact, the Indian and Senegalese ventures were more complicated than simply efforts on the part of the Iranian company to sell oil. Iran envisioned supplies of iron ore from India and phosphates from Senegal in exchange for its oil.

It is difficult to predict from which end of the chain vertical integration will begin when there are advantages to linking raw material sources closely with users. In a number of cases, the integration has been undertaken when a raw materials supplier has acquired outlets. Autlan of Mexico, for example, has plants in Alabama and Venezuela that serve as outlets for Mexican minerals. In another case, Copersucre, a Brazilian sugar cooperative, acquired control of Hills Brothers, a U.S. coffee roaster. The original intent, according to managers interviewed in connection with this research, was to obtain access to Hills Brothers's coffee distribution systems so that it could be used for sugar sales. Unexpectedly, the need for outlets disappeared as Brazil's energy programs generated a rapid growth in demand for sugar to be made into alcohol for fuel. A North African investment in Europe had similar goals. Algerian exporters of dates found that French packers had mastered market knowledge and held control over outlets in France. They would, according to Algerians, buy only unprocessed dates. The Algerian response was to acqure a Marseille packer. Algerians hoped that closer ties to the market would enable them eventually to export processed dates from their country.[34]

In a few cases, the need for vertical integration has led to the establishment of a manufacturing project in a third country, one that is neither the source of materials nor the principal market for the products. For example, a Brazilian enterprise joined with Maltese and Libyan interests for a plant in Malta to process Brazilian timber for European and Arab markets.[35]

The history of U.S. and European firms that have sought raw materials abroad suggests that some such firms become much more international than their original moves might have suggested. After the major oil companies went to the Middle East, they began to seek markets other than those at home where they could dispose of their large quantities of oil. Eventually, dependence on one or two sources of oil looked risky, so they sought sources in other countries. Then more markets were required. One sees bits and pieces of such patterns already emerging in a few firms from developing countries, whether their vertical integration started from market or materials. For example, an Argentine firm, Industrias Siderurgias Grassi S.A., went to Brazil to secure a source of inexpensive manganese alloys for steel. To make full use of the output of the new facility, however, it needed a larger market than it had at home. Thus, it also disposed of its product in Brazil, the rest of Latin America, Europe, and the United States. In another case, the National Iranian Oil Company has thought of diversifying its sources of oil. Before the Iranian revolution, it was apparently considering joining British Petroleum in the North Sea, having already participated in refining in other countries.[36]

In their strategies for vertical integration, most companies involved in raw materials differ from the manufacturing firms that are the principal subject of this book. Their foreign operations do not necessarily involve the transfer of special skills or knowledge. In some ways they are much like the banks. For certain industries there are advantages associated with extracting raw materials and processing them within the same enterprise. When the raw materials lie in one country and the efficient site for processing is located in another country, a firm becomes international to take advantage of the gains associated with vertical integration. The trigger is likely to be difficulty in obtaining reliable inputs of raw materials if the firm is first engaged in manufacturing; if the firm begins with the production of the raw material, the trigger is the problem in disposing of output on a regular basis or on attractive terms.

To be sure, an occasional foreign raw materials venture of a parent from a developing country seems to be the result of something other than the search for a secure supply, reliable markets, or even technology. In Venezuela and Ecuador, a Peruvian company is operating small mines. It seems that no multinational was interested in the small-scale projects, but the Peruvian firm was accustomed to such operations. In Haiti, a Peruvian geologist proposed that a test tunnel for a potential copper mine be constructed by a South American firm. The North American mining firms, he claimed, have forgotten how to dig small, narrow test tunnels. With their high labor costs, such firms use automatic equipment and make wide cuts. What was called for was the use of local cheap labor to dig a crude, inexpensive access to explore the extent of the deposit, something that U.S. firms were unwilling to do but which South American firms would undertake. In these unusual cases, skills are involved that are similar to those transferred by manufacturing firms.

A few rare raw material investments by firms from developing countries seem to be similar to construction activities in that the investing firm holds a competitive advantage through its access to cheap factors of production. For example, Philippine timber firms that have established several operations in Indonesian Borneo (Kalimantan) appear to have little that is special in the way of technology, with the possible exception of familiarity with working in virgin tropical forests and in conditions where it is difficult to bring in heavy equipment. The accounting flexibility of such firms and the lack of regulation at home do make it easier for them than for U.S. and European firms to operate in a sector particularly known for corruption in Southeast Asia. Although these differences are helpful, the principal advantage of the Philippine timbering firms is access to trained labor. As accessible timber resources in the Philippines have become depleted, excess skilled labor has become available. In contrast, skilled labor is not easily available in sparsely settled Borneo, in spite of the general high level of unemployment in Indonesia. Thus, Philippine firms have exported their timbering crews virtually intact over the short distance to Indonesia. The profits, they report, are extraordinary.

Conclusions

There have been few studies of the international spread of nonmanufacturing firms, whatever their original origins. Previous work and this study suggest certain patterns, however.

The international spread of some service firms, like that of manufacturing firms, is based on the possession of certain advantages. The advantages to be used abroad are sometimes technological, deriving from conditions in the home market; sometimes the advantages are associated with brand names. Nonmanufacturing firms that go abroad do not, however, possess clearly identifiable skills or brand names in the usual sense. Perhaps peculiar to firms from developing countries, some companies have access to labor that can be used abroad. For more firms, internationalization results from the gains that accrue only from capturing within the same enterprise certain activities that can be efficiently carried out in different countries. They are similar to the manufacturing firms that have established assembly plants in the industrialized countries for components produced at home.

Unlike the usual manufacturing firms, whose skills originate from the conditions of the home market, the banks and raw material firms could begin from either rich or poor countries. Banks may internationalize to serve importers or exporters. Firms may begin the process of vertical integration from the raw material end or the user end. Domestic experience in the advanced countries suggests that the user is more likely to integrate backward into sources. Nevertheless, the direction of integration may have to do more with the historic availability of capital and management and, in some cases, colonial policies than with any of the modern theories of multinational enterprises.

Once a few firms have begun the process of integration, other firms are likely to follow suit to protect their positions. But when firms have established a dominant position, whether beginning as raw materials ventures or as users, newcomers are likely to be at a disadvantage. Thus, well established international banks or vertically integrated raw material firms from the advanced countries have the advantage of experience. In recent years, however, some firms from developing countries have had the resources to take the first steps toward internationalization when new trade routes opened up. In other cases, nationalizations of established firms have provided opportunities for banks or raw material enterprises from the developing countries to establish international networks. Some of the internationalization of firms from developing countries, however, may be too late to be helpful to the enterprises involved. In some industries, companies may be emulating the old patterns of multinationals from the industrialized countries at a time when the industries have changed so much that there are few benefits left from internationalization. In raw materials, for example, when there are many suppliers and a large fraction are not part of vertically integrated enterprises, contractual arrangements may serve to secure suppliers of materials as well as would direct investment.

9   Government Policies

Julius Nyerere, Tanzania's president, has been quoted as wanting "Third World multinational corporations owned by us and controlled by us to serve our purposes."[1] Like Nyerere, others are attracted to foreign investments between developing countries as sources of appropriate technology without some of the economic and political costs associated with the acquisition of technology from the industrialized countries. In spite of the hopes, neither host nor home governments have unanimously favored the expansion of the kinds of firms included in this study.

Host Governments

Government policies of host countries have ranged from encouragement to discouragement. Sri Lanka, Mauritius, and Papua New Guinea have all recruited investors from Hong Kong, largely for the economic advantages. The policies of the Egyptian government have favored Arab investors over other foreign investors, principally to further Arab unity.[2] On paper at least, the members of the Andean Common Market in Latin America prefer investors from other Latin American countries partly as a counterweight to the powerful economic and political position held by the United States.

In spite of the attractions, foreign investment, whether from developing countries or elsewhere, raises sensitive economic and political issues, such as transfer pricing, effects on local entrepreneurship, and fear of domination by others. The concerns are reflected in restrictive policies. Indonesia and Nepal, for example, have imposed special restrictions on investors from certain other developing countries. Indonesian authorities have, on occasion, been hesitant to approve investment proposals offered by firms from Singapore and Hong Kong.

Simple economic factors seem to play a much smaller role than sensitivity to the presence of ethnic Chinese businessmen in their reluctance to accept applications from these countries. Similarly, Nepal, fearing Indian domination, prefers investors from less politically sensitive sources. A number of investors from developing countries have faced forced sales or expropriations of their foreign subsidiaries.

At times, bureaucratic procedures of host governments can put investors from developing countries at a disadvantage compared to multinationals from the rich countries. When the choice lies between a well-known American, European, or Japanese firm and a relatively unknown firm from another developing country, the risk-averse government official may well see the selection of the well-known firm as involving less danger to his career. After all, if Dow, Union Carbide, or Hoechst fails to get a chemical project off the ground, the fault is unlikely to lie with the official's choice of firms, or so it might seem.

With no intention of doing so, many governments discourage investors from other developing countries through their formal approval procedures. Small investors are hindered by cumbersome administrative steps that require applicants to spend a long time in the country for negotiations or that entail many trips to visit the country before investment takes place. The small firm is particularly unlikely to be able to spare managers to continue extensive negotiations at government convenience. Because it usually must spread the fixed costs of entry over a smaller project, the small firm is likely to find long negotiations more burdensome than is the large firm. Since foreign investors from developing countries are likely to be small firms, they are particularly hard hit by such entry procedures.

The analysis in this book has suggested some solid economic factors that argue for foreign investors from developing countries.

The kind of technology transferred by the typical manufacturer should be a prime consideration. Small-scale technology means higher capacity utilization for the host country. It also means more employment than the rich-country multinational usually offers and, according to skimpy data, more than is offered by the typical local entrepreneur. Further, the technology supplied by the developing country investor means less imported inputs and correspondingly greater development of local supplies.

Host countries should also consider the marketing strategies of the Third World investors. First, their lack of emphasis on advertising reduces some the concern that foreign investors transmit alien cultural

Table 9.1
Royalties/technical fees paid by foreign subsidiaries to Indian parents

Royalties/technical fees paid to parents	Number of subsidiaries
Limited time period between 1–7 years	
2–3% sales	10
Fixed sum per year	2
Unlimited time period	
2% sales	4
10% sales	2
One-time flat fee (not on sales)	10
(from Rs. 1 lakh–Rs. 1 million)	
Amount of fee unknown	2
No fees	8

Source: Interviews conducted by Carlos Cordeiro.

values. Perhaps more significant, the tendency of such firms to compete on price is particularly needed in countries where import protection and small markets lead to few producers of a given product.

The notable tendency of developing country investors to share ownership with local partners is likely to appeal to some host countries. Whatever the actual value of local ownership, its political appeal remains great.[3] The autonomy given by most such firms to subsidiaries will also have its attractions.

Some hints, not previously mentioned, suggest that developing country investors may save more foreign exchange for the host country than do investors from the industrialized countries. One source of savings, of course, is the tendency of firms from developing countries to acquire inputs locally. Another comes from apparently lower payments to parents in the form of royalties and dividends, although the evidence is only suggestive. Comparative information on royalties available from Thailand showed that the average multinational from an industrialized country paid 3 percent of sales as royalty and the average investor from another developing country paid only 0.2 percent.[4] Figures also showed that Indian-owned subsidiaries, wherever they are located, also generally paid low royalties. Many paid a lump sum at the outset. Two that paid on a sales basis paid more than 3 percent of sales (table 9.1)

The reader familiar with studies of U.S.-based multinationals might find the conclusions to be somewhat surprising, since royalty payments by affiliates of U.S. firms are known to be inversely related to ownership. For the U.S. multinationals, joint ventures pay more royalties than wholly owned subsidiaries, probably because all the profits of a wholly owned subsidiary accrue to the parent. In such cases, the choice of label for dividends or royalties is largely a matter of the implications for tax or foreign exchange control regulations. Since most of the overseas affiliates of the firms from developing countries operate as joint ventures, one might expect, on average, higher royalty payments for them than for the U.S.-based firms. In actuality, joint ventures from developing countries pay less, and the explanation for this may lie in the fact that technology provided by the firms from developing countries is more widely available than that provided by enterprises from the advanced countries.

Sketchy information on profit remissions to the parent firm also suggests the possibility of additional foreign exchange savings associated with investors from developing countries. In Thailand, subsidiaries of traditional multinationals report annual profit remissions of 27 percent of their equity, while foreign investors from developing countries show only 3.7 percent. The figures could reflect higher rates of earning by the traditional multinationals; however, evidence from another study by the same author found no statistically significant difference between the profits of 23 firms from developing countries.[5] In Thailand, the firms from developing countries reported a *higher* return on investment than did the advanced country investors. For this study, no data on profit remissions were collected. Even though there are few data, there are reasons to expect that the remissions of firms from developing countries may be low in many countries, whatever the profits. Given the role that foreign investments play in diversifying the pool of assets held by owners of the parent firms, it is quite possible that many enterprises retain a large portion of their earnings abroad.

Most foreign investors from developing countries have little in the way of export markets to offer, since home markets are small and are usually highly protected through tariffs and other barriers. Offshore manufacturers, however, are one obvious, and important, class of exceptions to the general rule on export markets. Although they accounted for only a small fraction of the firms identified in this study, they can play a disproportionately large role in the development process. If a government wants to develop a sector that manufactures for export, foreign investors from other developing countries offer a way to begin.[6] The problem facing a country with no exporters in a particular industry is how to establish contact and a good reputation with buyers from the advanced countries. Many such contacts are made through visits of buyers, who assess the managers and the plants of prospective suppliers. Buyers are, however, reluctant to visit and spend time in a country that has not proved its ability to supply. The task for a government that wants to create a sector, then, is to get the process started. Investors from established exporting countries offer an opportunity. The interviews suggest that buyers initially contract only through the parent enterprise but eventually visit the foreign subsidiaries. Once the buyers come, local firms have the opportunity to contact them and demonstrate their skills.

What some host countries and most academics view as advantageous product and process technology is viewed by other host countries as a negative factor associated with developing country investors. In spite of the fashions, governments in many developing countries want the most advanced technology. Anything that might be small in scale or labor-intensive is easily associated with out-of-date, inefficient know-how that is unlikely to lead to modern skills and success in export markets. Even though the firms in this study are far from the kinds of tiny enterprises proposed in *Small is Beautiful*,[7] they are viewed by some policy makers in the same light. Even if a government views the technology as appropriate, it might be concerned about the speed with which it is transferred to nationals. The heavy reliance of developing country investors on expatriate managers and technicians indicates that transfer is not rapid.

There are other negative factors associated with developing country investments. First, anecdotal evidence indicates that the foreign investor from a developing country is even more likely to be involved in questionable payments to government officials than is the firm from an industrialized country. Managers of developing country firms suggested that such payments are easier when managers are related, when the firm is small, when bookkeeping is informal, and when the parent faces no home government controls, such as those imposed in the United States under the Foreign Corrupt Practices Act.

Second, there is some evidence that foreign investors from developing countries are particularly likely to locate in the largest cities of their host countries. These are, of course, where crowding is already a problem. The tendency should not be surprising. A strategy of short runs of varied products and low advertising leads a firm to need very close contact with its major market. Further, small firms are unlikely to be able to afford a second office near the government center to handle bureaucratic measures, so important in most developing countries. Locating the plant near such a center means that the same managers can handle production and government relations.

Although the typical foreign investor from a developing country may be quite different from the multinational firm from an industrialized country, a government hosting foreign investment will, often enough, view the two kinds of investors as alternatives for a given project. In such cases, host governments must decide which kind of investor is more appropriate for a given project or what combination of investors would provide a suitable mix for a particular industrial sector. Moreover, promotion activities and incentives can be designed to influence the mix of investors in a country.

The results of this research indicate that the net benefits of firms of one kind do not consistently outweigh the net benefits of the other kind. The choice must take into account the host country's objectives. Moreover, when the choice is between encouraging foreign investors from other developing countries and firms from the advanced countries, the broad generalizations can only serve to direct the decision maker to areas where differences are likely. No group of foreign investors is homogeneous. Nevertheless, my own suspicion is that investors from other developing countries offer, on average, more net benefits for most host countries than do the traditional multinationals, except when the traditional firms bring access to significant export markets.

Perhaps in the majority of cases, government officials are, in fact, not faced with the kind of choice just posed. The official has a proposal in front of him. Uncertain of all the merits of the proposal at hand, the official might want to seek alternatives. If the available proposal is unappealing because of the kind of technology to be used or the degree of foreign control, for example, some of the investors of the kind dealt with in this book could be more attractive and might be courted.

In some situations, investors from advanced countries and investors from other developing countries are not alternatives at all. In most high-technology industries, such as for computer hardware or commercial aircraft manufacture, there are no potential investors from developing countries. Similarly, for some industries there are few or no multinationals from the advanced countries, perhaps none for enamel pots and pans, Chinese noodles, and charcoal-fired steel plants, and perhaps relatively few for paper packaging or spinning and weaving.

In the case of the offshore manufacturers, firms from other developing countries invest in industries that do not attract many investors from the advanced countries, such as in the garment and canvas shoe industries. In those cases, the firms from the richer countries see little advantage in internalizing the transactions and are perfectly satisfied with simple purchasing arrangements. On the other hand, the developing country firm has a need to internalize its purchases and thus invests abroad.

Even when alternative investors from the industrialized countries exist, the comparison often misses the burning issues that face officials when they are considering proposals from the kinds of firms studied in this book. The greatest cost posed by investors from other developing countries is likely to be that they might preempt exactly those kinds of opportunities that local firms would soon take up in the absence of foreign investment. The choice appears to be between a project from another developing country now or a similar one generated by a local firm at some additional cost and at a later date. There are, of course, no simple answers in this kind of choice.

When the alternatives do involve firms of different nationalities, the host country is likely to benefit from the presence of several potential investors. The growth in the number of foreign investors from developing countries means that there are more firms offering skills for many kinds of activity. Common sense and recent evidence argue that the presence of a larger number of potential investors for a particular kind of project is likely to result in a better deal for the host country.[8] In the end it may be that this is the most significant impact of such firms for the poorer developing countries.

Host countries that want to encourage more investment from developing countries for the skills they bring or for the increased bargaining powers associated with their interest, can make the investment terms more attractive. Tariff rates on capital equipment can be lowered if the equipment comes from other developing countries. Restrictions can be lifted on the import of second-hand machinery. Sectors closed to most foreign investors might be kept open to investors from other developing countries (as Egypt has done for Arab investors). Favored investors can be exempted from rules requiring scheduled increases in local ownership, as has happened in the Andean group. Tax incentives might even be considered, but cautiously. Although they seem to have little impact on the decisions of firms from advanced countries, it is quite possible that they prove attractive to investors from developing countries. Since many such investors pay no tax at home on foreign earnings, tax incentives in host countries result in a financial benefit to the firm. There are bilateral possibilities as well. Sri Lanka, for example, has already negotiated a tax treaty and has considered negotiating a bilateral insurance treaty with Singapore to cover investors from that country.[9]

Policies such as these probably have only very limited effects. The most effective actions are those that are most difficult. Some countries, as has been mentioned, have recruited foreign investors by sending missions to countries that are potential sources; for example, Mauritius and Papua New Guinea have gone to Hong Kong, and Sri Lanka has gone to India. If the programs are carefully targeted and designed to recognize the motivations of investors, they can work, according to officials involved. Probably the most effective but most difficult action would be the simplification of the procedures and the acceleration of decisions concerning investment approvals.

Home Governments

Attitudes of home governments have been almost as diverse as those of host governments. Some countries, such as Mexico and Hong Kong, require no approval for their firms to invest abroad. Others require potential investors to obtain permits. Some lay down fairly explicit rules. The Indian government requires its firms to enter joint ventures when they go abroad and in the past required them to limit their contribution to Indian machinery and to export no foreign exchange.[10] Each project is approved separately by the Indian government. The Korean and Taiwan governments also require their firms to seek approval for each project so that the economic benefits for the home country can be examined. In the analysis, the focus of most home governments appears to be on any exports that a project might generate from the home country or any access to raw materials needed at home. Taiwan regulations state that outward investments must meet one of the following requirements: promote the sales of domestic products; make available raw materials required by domestic industries; expand the market for the products of the investor whose domestic plant has excess capacity; be conducive to the export of technical know-how that may increase foreign exchange earnings; or promote international economic cooperation.[11]

Although Latin American governments vary in the scrutiny they give proposals, most South American countries require approval of investment through their exchange control procedures. Peru not only requires approval of outgoing investments through the same institution that is responsible for incoming investments but requires permits for the export of used machinery from the country. Brazil, like many other countries, seems to smile only on projects that support exports or that hold the promise of providing raw materials.

Once countries have granted approval, they may even grant incentives to their investors. Typical incentives include exemption from home taxes and the provision of guarantees for loans associated with the export of machinery manufactured at home.[12]

The economic case for foreign manufacturing investment from the home country's point of view is a mixed one. The biggest costs, according to the governments, are the foreign exchange outflows at the beginning of an investment. Some countries also fear that overseas subsidiaries open potential leaks in the exchange control systems. With a base outside the country, a firm can find various ways of evading exchange controls at home. Although foreign investment initially means, in most cases, an outflow of foreign exchange from the home country, overseas activities should eventually earn exchange in the form of dividends and fees. They may generate exports in the form of materials and complementary products that would not otherwise have been sold. The story given by an Indian manager was reminiscent of reports on U.S. investment abroad. The manager pointed out that the foreign investments were important for his firm in establishing a reputation for his company overseas. This reputation helped in exporting products complementary to what the company was manufacturing in its foreign subsidiaries.

Foreign investment requires the export of managerial and technical personnel as well as foreign exchange. Such personnel may have an opportunity cost at home. On the other hand, some of the interviews have supported the claim that the opportunity cost is low in family-held firms. Managers sent overseas may be underemployed at home, and their foreign experience may provide them with general management training that has a long-run benefit for the home country.

Export of machinery is usually of little worry to home governments. When investment consists of locally made machinery or second-hand equipment, that machinery has, in many cases, little opportunity cost for the home country. There may be no domestic use for it, and given the poorly developed markets for new machinery from developing countries and for used equipment of all types, it might not be exported in the absence of investment.

Home governments fear that foreign investments will displace exports of final goods, but the data on motivations for investment suggest that investment is undertaken primarily when exports are threatened. Many of the exports would probably disappear regardless of whether the investment is undertaken.

The political issues for home countries concerning foreign investment are complex. Some countries, such as India, are likely to be concerned that it will strengthen the largest enterprises in the country, those that matter in antitrust policy. Relations with neighboring countries can be improved or weakened by foreign investment. When the home country is already viewed as a dominant political power, or its nationals have become successful immigrants abroad, the effects might well be negative. On the other hand, investments might be seen by neighbors as useful ways to loosen their dependence on more powerful countries of the North. The results are likely to be quite different from country to country. Generalizations are of little value.

Sufficient data on foreign investments are simply not available to determine the net impact of the associated costs and benefits on the home country. Given the importance of constraints of foreign exchange and skilled managers to developing countries, most governments will probably continue to screen proposed foreign investments, approving only those that promise quick payoffs in the form of exports. There are strong hints, however, that many firms will find a way to invest abroad with or without approval at home. Published data from host countries sometimes report considerably more investment from restrictive home countries than those home countries have approved (see appendix). Moreover, the interviews uncovered quite a few foreign investments that had been undertaken without the knowledge of home governments, even though regulations required reporting. There is no reason to anticipate that in the future firms will be more responsive to restrictions.

International Institutions

Although governments of developing countries have mixed attitudes toward foreign investments by their firms, certain international organizations unequivocally support "developing-country joint ventures." This support derives from several characteristics of Third World multinationals. The International Labour Office, for instance, is especially interested in the possibilities of job creation that are associated with the kinds of technology transferred by the firms. The U.N. organizations are most interested in the role that such firms can play in developing self-reliance among the countries of the South and are very concerned with what they see as the dependency of the developing countries on the rich North for technology required for development. As an example of South-South cooperation, Third World multinationals provide a live model for other cooperative efforts that hold out promise of economic and political benefits for the developing nations.[13]

Regional organizations see contributions that developing country firms can make to economic and political integration within their regions and more obvious benefits from appropriate technology and appropriate products. In the hope of encouraging investments within their regions, some groups have taken concrete steps. The Andean group has adopted special provisions (Decision 46) to encourage the development of regional enterprises. SELA, the Latin American Economic System founded in 1975, and the Central American Common Market have both indicated similar interests in regional firms.[14] INTAL (Instituto para la Integración de America Latina) has long promoted the idea of "joint enterprises" in Latin America because they are thought to encourage integration among the area's economies.

In their deliberations, policy makers in some development organizations and in the regional organizations have conceived of a rather special kind of project for regional investment. The idealized concept is of a newly created enterprise that is jointly owned by nationals of different countries but not the "subsidiary" of any one parent. Consistent with this concept, the model suggested by some international organizations does not place emphasis on the flow of technology from an existing enterprise to a new one, its subsidiary.

Although the idealized model is attractive for political reasons, few of the investments actually encountered in this study correspond to the type. Most of the exceptional cases that did fit the idealized description were the creation of two or more governments. Most are for infrastructure, particularly power generation and navigation projects, such as those undertaken by Paraguay and Argentina and Paraguay and Brazil. Most such projects that have gone beyond the planning stage have been in Latin America.

The Merchant Fleet Grancolombiana S.A. illustrates one kind of joint project desired by the regional organizations. Started in 1946 for shipping, it involved the National Federation of Colombian Coffee Growers, the National Development Bank of Ecuador, the National Sailing Company of Colombia, and the Agriculture and Cattle Bank of Venezuela, all state-owned entities. The resulting Colombia-based merchant fleet was to provide a regional fleet for primary exports. The history has been checkered, with Venezuela withdrawing in 1953. Profits have been reported for only a few years.

A few regional projects have been for manufacturing. In such cases, the technology has generally come from a firm based in an industrialized country.[15]

Monomeros, another example of the type of venture desired by international organizations, is an enterprise established in Colombia by IVP, a Venezuelan state-owned enterprise; Ecopetrol, a Colombian state firm; IFI, a Colombian development finance institution; and DSM-Stamicarbon N.V., a Colombian subsidiary of a Dutch state enterprise. The venture was started to use IVP's ammonia, Dutch technology, and Colombian labor to produce fertilizer and an essential ingredient in the manufacture of nylon.

In Africa, there have been proposals for similar multinational ventures without a clear parent-subsidiary relationship. For example, Nigeria and Benin have discussed a joint cement project and plans for acquiring technology from Europe. The original plans for Ciments de l'Afrique de l'Ouest (CIMAO), another proposed venture involving primarily governments, was to include a cement plant and a clinker plant in Togo, clinker plants in Upper Volta and the Ivory Coast, and rehabilitated cement plants in the Ivory Coast and Benin. Eventually, Ghana and Niger were to be included. By 1975, the potential participants were down to Togo, the Ivory Coast, and Ghana. The project, like many similar ones, seems never to have come into being.[16]

The history of such joint projects suggests that they will remain the exceptions. When the economics strongly favor joint infrastructure development, joint efforts have some record of success, but few such projects for manufacturing and other industrial activities have succeeded. Absent has been the critical drive of a motivated entrepreneur, either private or public.

International organizations, nevertheless, probably have a significant role to play in the development of enterprises of the type that are more common. In several cases, they have provided the initial information that led to investment. The International Finance Corporation brought investment opportunities to the attention of some of the firms identified in this study and has put up its money to help some projects. The reports and political pressures from international organizations can encourage governments to remove some of the barriers to the establishment of foreign subsidiaries by firms from developing countries; they can also assist new investors in learning from the experience of firms that have already invested abroad. INTAL, for example, has had lawyers examine the legal problems encountered by Latin American firms that invest in other countries in the region and has recommended changes in national legislation as a result. Further, it has provided details to prospective investors about the ways existing investors have structured their projects to minimize problems.

Governments of Industrialized Countries

Governments of industrialized countries do not have explicit policies toward foreign investors from developing countries. The investment flows do, however, affect their interests, even though they are hosts to few subsidiaries. The firms have an impact on the development process in the poor countries, which is a matter of concern to the rich nations. Further, they affect the operations of international firms based in the industrialized countries.

Since foreign investors from developing countries are a new source of competition for their own firms, governments in the rich countries might well view with alarm the emergence of such investors, regardless of any favorable impact on the development process. The effect of that competition, however, is likely to be uneven. Firms that offer technology near the end of the product cycle are the most severely affected, and those that specialize in spinning and weaving, construction work, and other activities that have been mastered by firms in this study are the most threatened. Without the foreign investors from developing countries, such firms might be able to exploit their know-how a bit longer. In some cases, the firms most affected are those that have entered international markets late, with relatively little advantage of their own. A significant portion of the effect of the new competition is likely to fall on European and Japanese firms. The data indicate that they, and the smaller U.S. firms, are more like the firms from the developing countries than are the usual large American multinationals.

For some of the multinationals from the advanced countries that rely on marketing techniques to differentiate their products and obtain higher margins, the emergence of investors from developing countries poses a new kind of challenge. In the past, multinationals faced only local firms that competed on price in, say, detergents or flashlight batteries. Now, there are foreign investors spreading through the developing countries that are able to struggle with the multinationals over the price-sensitive segment of the markets.

The new international firms also provide some opportunities for certain multinationals from the advanced countries. They are attractive partners for projects in third countries. In this study, we identified 73 manufacturing subsidiaries that were jointly owned by parents from other developing countries and parents from advanced countries.

Cooperative arrangements fall into three categories. First, in a number of cases multinationals from the advanced countries have provided marketing skills (usually embodied partly in a brand name), while partners from developing countries have provided knowledge of operating in developing countries and relevant technological know-how.

Second, in several cases a multinational from Europe or the United States has encouraged a firm from a developing country with which it had had previous relations to take up an opportunity in a third country. No joint ownership need be involved, but the multinational could hope for sales of equipment or materials to the new operation. When such contacts were identified in this study, they involved projects that might turn out to be too small to justify the high cost of management time from the multinational but might be quite suitable for the lower overhead costs of a developing country associate. Packages Limited, for example, was led to Indonesia (a management arrangement) by its original Swedish technology supplier.

In a third and rare type of arrangement, a multinational from an industrialized country has joined with a firm from a developing country to build an international system of vertically integrated activities. One case of a complex strategy of vertical integration involved a Hong Kong firm, a Japanese firm, and several Southeast Asian affiliates. Textile Alliance, Ltd. (T.A.L.), in Hong Kong, started as a pooling of some interests of a Chinese entrepreneur and Jardine Matheson. When T.A.L.'s future seemed in doubt due to financial problems, Toray acquired almost half the shares of T.A.L. between 1971 and 1978. Not only was a customer kept in business but an international strategy was instituted. According to managers interviewed for this study, T.A.L. provided spinning and weaving knowledge, and less widely available, knowledge of garment making. The managers point out that there are schools for textile engineering but no equivalent for garment making. Toray provided synthetic fibers. Since it needed steady sales to spread its fixed costs, Toray could benefit from a captive customer, especially during the frequent periods of surplus capacity. Vertical integration would serve a role similar to that which it has served for aluminum firms.

The emerging strategy of the T.A.L. system seems, to an outsider, to be built around a pattern that goes something as follows: A network of affiliated garment plants is established in Southeast Asian markets. At the outset, the textiles are purchased from T.A.L., which in turn uses Toray fiber. When import controls appear imminent or another manufacturer threatens to preempt the market by establishing a weaving plant, T.A.L. moves in with its own weaving facilities, still using Toray's fibers from Japan. Spinning is likely to be the next stage. Finally, when the continued import of synthetic fibers is threatened, a Toray affiliate is established to manufacture the fibers locally. By 1978, the strategy had led to a large network of T.A.L. affiliates: at least five subsidiaries in Taiwan, five in Malaysia, two in Mauritius, one in Singapore, one in Thailand, one in Indonesia, and one in Nigeria. Toray held directly an interest in T.A.L. subsidiaries in Thailand, Malaysia, and Singapore.[17]

In the long run, the most important impact of developing country investors on the advanced countries may have nothing to do with the competition and opportunities described thus far. Rather, it may come from the blurring of the distinction between governments that are hosts and governments that are homes to foreign investors. A few years ago, countries such as India, Brazil, and Mexico viewed themselves as hosts, usually reluctant ones, to foreign investors. Today, they are hosts to firms from the industrialized countries and also home countries to a new generation of international firms as well.

The history of European attitudes toward foreign investments suggests that changes such as those in the more advanced developing countries will have an impact on attitudes of governments. European criticism of American multinationals has softened considerably with the expansion of European multinationals. I would bet on the same kind of changes in the developing countries when their own firms become significant investors abroad. Indeed, an Indian government memo suggests that the emergence of Indian multinationals has already had its effects:

As India is emerging as an exporter of enterprise and capital equipment which form the basis for our joint ventures abroad, it is important to be circumspect as regards the treatment we mete out to foreign enterprises and foreigners doing business with and in India. . . . Not only

[may] such foreign capital and technology that we would like to attract in the interest of speedy economic growth not be forthcoming, but our own industries and business interests abroad may face similar disabilities.[18]

Changed attitudes on the part of governments open up numerous possibilities for international agreements on foreign investments. Transfer pricing, large investment incentives, and performance requirements on foreign firms (such as minimum export levels) are the kinds of issues that vex governments with international business transactions. They are the kinds of issues that are more likely to be amenable to international treaties as governments lose their identity as being consistently on one side or the other of investment flows. Many serious proposed solutions to such problems appear to host countries as favoring home countries; home countries view the same solutions as favoring host countries. Solutions are more likely to be accepted if government interests are more balanced.

Whatever one concludes about the merits of developing country investors for the advanced countries, one might conclude that governments of these countries have no influence in the matter. Although their potential impact is indeed quite limited, certain policies can have some effect. The primary vehicles for influence are through aid programs and international organizations.

To the extent that aid from the advanced countries is tied only to sources outside the developing world, it fails to promote South-South investment or trade that eventually leads to such investments. In one case with which I am familiar, a developing country sought assistance from the aid agency of a European country to establish a hoe factory. The aid agency insisted on procurement of know-how from the European nation. More appropriate technology for such a simple product could have probably been obtained from another developing country.

Although untied aid might be the optimal policy from the point of view of the developing countries, restrictions that limit purchase either to the aid provider or to other developing countries would be an improvement over strict ties to the aid giver. The results would be some encouragement to foreign investments within the developing countries. In fact, such policies do seem to be catching on.

Although the influence of the advanced countries is not great in most of the regional organizations, it is significant in certain worldwide entities. The International Finance Corporation, one such organization, was identified several times in this study as having provided the initial information that led to foreign investments. In some cases, it has been involved in the financing of subsidiaries of developing country investors. With its wide sources of information and its understanding of the motivations of private firms, it provides an obvious vehicle for encouraging such investments.

10   Prospects for the Firms

To end this book with unambiguous enthusiasm for what direct investment from one developing country to another can contribute to development and to forecast a rosy future for the firms themselves would be misleading. Although a simple projection of recent data might indicate that an investor is likely to do very well, there are some indications that suggest a more cautious forecast.

The first suggestion of future difficulty is the history of some of the early foreign investors. Several of the pioneering firms from Argentina have not continued to expand abroad. S.I.A.M. di Tella has sold its foreign operations. Alpargatas, another early Argentine investor, has held onto its Brazilian affiliate, but its stake in ownership now is very small, and the headquarters seems to exercise little control over the Brazilian firm. Moreover, new ideas are as likely to be transferred from the Brazilian Alpargatas to the Argentine firm as they are to be transferred from the parent to the affiliate. More recent Indian data also suggest mixed success on the part of Indian foreign investors. The failure rate for overseas subsidiaries seems to be extraordinarily high. India is perhaps the only country that reports data indicating failure rates, but even without official figures, there is no doubt that investing firms from other developing countries have had difficulties.

Some of the firms that failed went abroad without any particular advantages and found the net costs of operating as a foreign enterprise too heavy to bear. Many of the firms that went abroad with advantages failed after a short time because of the nature of the advantages they exploited.

Manufacturing Firms

The firms interviewed for this study had survived abroad for some period, usually with an identifiable advantage. Their experience with certain technologies at home gave them advantages over local firms in other countries that were less developed than their home country. Moreover, they met little challenge from the firms of rich countries as long as they stayed on their own turf. But here is the rub. Although their experience at home gave them advantages over local firms, in most cases it would be a matter of only a few years until local firms could copy their skills or develop similar skills. Rarely were the advantages of the firms in this study protected by patents or by barriers in the form of large investments in research and development that would give the firms protection from competition.

If a foreign investor's initial advantage is captured by others, the firm can follow several paths. Multinationals such as IBM have simply rolled over their product lines and technology as competitive advantages have been eroded in old lines. Other advanced country firms have dug in their heels by spending heavily on marketing to differentiate their products in the minds of consumers. In other cases, multinationals from the advanced countries have sought low manufacturing costs by increasing the scale of their plants. The approach has been to integrate manufacturing operations across countries to obtain economies of scale not available to any national producer. In still other cases, multinational firms from the advanced countries have not responded to the erosion of their initial competitive advantages and have lost their international positions. They lost market share to local firms; some sold their foreign subsidiaries.

Most foreign investors from the developing countries have, it would seem, few of these options. Only a small number of the firms identified in this study had continuing development activities that would lead to innovations to replace the old ones that local competitors had mastered. Large, diversified firms such as Tatung in Taiwan and the Birla Group of India illustrate the exceptional cases in which a continuing stream of innovations was generated.

Few firms from developing countries, as will be evident by now, have concentrated efforts on building trade names. Thus, most of these foreign investors do not have the skills to turn to product differentiation when their original technical skills no longer provide an adequate competitive advantage to counterbalance the costs of operating abroad. To be sure, as the more advanced developing countries become richer, many of their firms will probably turn their attention to trade names. By that time, however, it will probably be inappropriate to label the resulting enterprises "Third World multinationals"; their home countries will have joined the league of industrialized nations.

The strength of foreign investors from developing countries in relatively small-scale manufacture suggests that if their initial advantage were captured by others, it would be a rare firm that might try for large economies of scale by integrating operations across international borders. They have not done so thus far, and to do so would be to abandon a proven strength.

In sum, only a few enterprises have the strengths that would enable them to extend the lives of their subsidiaries once the initial advantages have been copied. As a result, the life cycles of many manufacturing subsidiaries of developing country firms will probably be short. With time, profits or market share are likely to be eroded by local competitors, ties with the original parent will weaken, and some subsidiaries will be sold by choice or through host government pressure.

A forecast of a relatively short life for many of the subsidiaries of firms from developing countries does not mean that overall investment flows will fall off. Indeed, the conditions that have produced the recent growth in investment seem likely to continue.

First, as long as firms from the richer developing countries gain experience that is later relevant for the next tier of countries, there will most probably be new firms with competitive advantages to take the places of those whose older advantages have eroded. Although an individual firm may not continue to grow abroad, its subsidiaries may be replaced by those of other firms with relevant advantages. This pattern of more advanced developing countries acting as technology filters for the lower tier countries is almost certain to continue and probably expand.

Second, the most common triggers to foreign investment by the investors in this study, threats to export markets, are likely to continue. The current interest in outward-looking development strategies in the Third World should assure a continued growth in trade of manufactured goods among developing countries. However, to the extent that developing countries do not erect barriers to imports, investment may not be a quick result. The firm with an advantage will continue to supply foreign markets by exporting. But, in spite of the popularity of more open borders, most poor countries continue to impose constraints on imports when the home market appears sufficiently large that the products could be manufactured locally at reasonable costs. Even countries with no serious foreign exchange constraints, such as Nigeria and

Indonesia, have continued their policies of restricting imports when local manufacture is feasible. As a result, there seems to be no reason to believe that the future will provide fewer triggers to investment than has the recent past.

Third, the drives for a firm to invest rather than to sell its advantages are also likely to continue. Foreign investment is only one possible response of a firm when its export markets are threatened. The firms in this study chose to internalize the process of transferring their advantages by establishing a subsidiary enterprise overseas because of the problems associated with contractual arrangements: difficulty of maintaining security, the imbalance of information between the seller and potential buyer of the advantage, and the many contingencies that would have to be built into a long-term arrangement. There seems to be no reason to expect that any of the problems accompanying contractual arrangements will diminish in the future.

As in the past, the dominant investment pattern will be from the more industrialized to the less industrialized countries. Few of the exportable advantages held by firms in this study are relevant in the richer countries. Small-scale manufacture, substitution of local materials, and other such skills are useful in the next lower tier of countries, where market conditions are similar to conditions that recently prevailed in the parent firm's home country.

The firms that have sought offshore sites to supply markets in the advanced countries have been exceptional cases throughout this study. They have been motivated largely by trade restrictions aimed at exports to the richer markets and by the need to obtain low-cost labor or, occasionally, raw materials as their costs at home have risen.

If trade restrictions expand in the advanced countries as imports from developing nations become more important, the incentives to seek quota-free sites will grow. Offshore investment is the likely result as long as the advanced countries impose quotas, "voluntary" or not, on a country by country basis. The investments will reflect the products that are at the time generating adjustment problems in the advanced countries. Moreover, higher incomes in the newly industrialized countries will almost certainly push more of their exporters to seek lower cost production sites in the lower wage countries. Thus, from the supply side, the environment appears favorable to the continued growth of foreign investment for offshore production.

Nevertheless, the future of such investments in any one country are bounded. As the last chapter pointed out, when firms in a particular country demonstrate their reliability and technical capabilities, buyers from the rich markets begin to visit that country. New national suppliers can grow. Consequently, a site such as Mauritius, which has depended on foreign investors for its entry into the export market for textiles, might well be able to expand its textile exports and move on to shoe manufacture and export without the participation of foreign firms. To be sure, when the technological gap is great, such as between shoes and electronics, foreign investment may still turn out to be the only reasonable way for such a country to gain both the know-how and access to new foreign markets. Nevertheless, a single country is likely to find a declining need over time for foreign-owned offshore plants from other developing countries in any one product line.

The conflicting influences on investment patterns are likely to mean that many developing country firms will establish new sites for manufacture, but the growth opportunities in any particular site or for any one product line are limited.

Nonmanufacturing Firms

The future of firms that attempt to establish vertically integrated systems, from raw material through processing, is also not secure. In a number of cases, companies from the developing countries that have attempted to integrate into the processing or marketing of their raw materials have done so only when the market was undergoing structural change. Change made entry easier, but it also made a strategy of vertical integration less attractive than it had been. When markets were under the control of the multinationals from the advanced countries, large barriers to entry were usually associated with a stage of the vertically integrated system. Thus, major multinational aluminum firms have held sway over operations from bauxite mining to fabrication largely because of the barriers to entry in smelting. The major oil countries have, at various times, maintained their oligopolistic positions through control over drilling technology or refining skills. Only when the barriers to entry have begun to fall have enterprises from developing countries attempted to replicate the vertical structures of the multinationals. Thus, the move of some state-owned oil enterprises from the developing countries into refining and distribution abroad has been the direct result of the fact that the oil market has slipped away from the grasp of the "Seven Sisters." With low barriers to entry and more diverse markets for the products, however, the advantages from vertical integration are likely to be smaller than in the past. Although vertical integration may yield somewhat more secure markets than those that face the firm that must sell on an open market, the new structures of industries such as oil are likely to mean fewer advantages and smaller profits than anticipated. As firms recognize that the strategies do not yield the monopoly profits that they associated with the old multinationals, they may well be less eager to attempt to emulate their predecessors.

A number of state-owned firms have gone abroad to obtain secure sources of raw materials for their home countries. The initial enthusiasm is again likely to be followed by some disillusionment. First, the moves abroad have, in most cases, occurred at a time when the power of the feared traditional multinational was already on the wane. Supplies of the needed materials have become increasingly available from a wide range of sources. Second, the experience of the advanced countries suggests that the loyalty of enterprises to their home countries is not as great as might be assumed, even when those enterprises are state-owned. Once the firms have a network of worldwide customers, in times of crisis they seem to show little preference for those of their own nationality.[1] To be sure, raw material firms from the developing countries do not yet have the complex international network of the traditional firms, but this study suggests that the successful ones will move in that direction.

Banks, accounting firms, hotels, and other service firms were given only cursory treatment in this study, so projections are particularly hazardous. Nevertheless, the role that the need to serve the international business of home customers plays in the expansion of some service firms, banks in particular, suggests some conclusions. I would expect their international expansion to continue in pace with the expansion of the international business of firms in their countries. Similarly, the best hotels in the more advanced developing countries are likely to find that their reputations are exploitable abroad as travelers from the advanced countries visit the home country frequently. In fact, some may find that business managers from the home country soon provide a significant customer base in nearby poorer nations.

Conclusions

The projections of this chapter and the arguments of the previous one are more tentative and less optimistic than I would have hoped when I began the study. But the growth of foreign investors from the developing countries is, it seems, no less complex than the growth of multinationals from the industrialized countries. After close to two decades of research on advanced country enterprises, observers still disagree on their effects and their future. Any conclusion rests heavily on judgment and on the point of view of the observer.

My own guess is that the spread of foreign investors from developing countries is, in net, beneficial to the development process and to international relations. Only part of that judgment is based on the narrow economic contributions of such firms.

The tensions between the rich countries of the North and the poor countries of the South run deep. No single phenomenon, such as the emergence of Third World multinationals, is going to cause those tensions to disappear. Nevertheless, foreign direct investment among the developing countries makes a contribution toward reducing those tensions. Much of the friction between North and South arises out of the dependency felt by the poor countries when they must turn to the rich for assets critical to their progress. The firms in this study reduce somewhat the dependency of the developing countries on the multinationals of the rich countries for much-needed technology, and I suspect that this benefits both rich and poor. In a world of reduced political tensions, decisions on foreign investment, whatever its national origin, are more likely to be made on sound economic grounds.

Appendix:
Data Sources

Probably the most complete tabulation of the official data on foreign investment flows among the developing countries is reported in a document of the U.N. Centre on Transnational Corporations.[1] Those figures are reproduced in table A.1. The data for Latin America have since been updated and expanded by INTAL.

Useful as these tabulations may be, they are far from complete. First, United Nations and INTAL data do not report separately on some very important suppliers and recipients of foreign investment. For Latin America, for example, there are no data on outflows from Mexico, apparently because the Mexican government does not collect such data. Second, no separate data are reported for India and Taiwan, although both countries publish reports on outflows.

The United Nations and other public data draw from official government sources, but there are many inconsistencies in official data from individual governments. One report in Thailand, for example, shows it as receiving $52 million in Taiwan investment during the 1970 and 1975 period.[2] The United Nations data just mentioned do not report separately on Taiwan investment in Thailand but show a total of only $22.1 million investment in Thailand from the "rest of Asia," which must include Taiwan. Further, Taiwan government figures show investment in Thailand of only $4.3 million.[3]

The reasons for such seeming contradictions in the data are several. One is the fact that various governments report quite different bits of information under similar rubrics. The most frequently used Indonesian data, for example, are for approved foreign investments. Many approved projects are never undertaken and others involve sums quite different from those reported in the application forms. On the other hand, the Philippine government, for example, appears to report actual investments. With numerous projects never being completed, the differences

Table A.1
Stock of foreign investment from Asian developing countries, as reported by host governments (1976)

Country of origin	Stock of foreign investment in host countries (× $1,000)				
	Thailand	Indonesia	Philippines	Hong Kong	Total
Hong Kong	10,900	728,300	14,200		753,400
India	2,400	19,400			21,800
Korea		107,400			107,400
Malaysia	5,000	42,700			47,700
Philippines	900	272,100		3,400	276,400
Singapore	2,200	115,600		13,400	131,200
Thailand				29,700	29,700
Other Asian developing countries	22,100	102,900	3,100	7,300	135,400
Total	43,500	1,388,400	17,300	53,800	1,503,000

Source: U.N. Centre on Transnational Corporations, *Transnational Corporations in World Development* (New York: United Nations, 1978), p. 247.

in reporting methods can be quite substantial. Some governments report only the amount of equity owned by foreigners; others report the total investment in projects in which foreigners have significant interests. The definition of direct investment differs from country to country. In Peru one project registered as Brazilian turned out to be so indicated because the founder's mother-in-law, a Brazilian, owned some shares. The founder claimed that the mother-in-law had no interest in managing the business affairs. In this case, the mother-in-law's claim to nonintervention seemed to be true. Moreover, some of the publicly available data include reinvested earnings. Further, some host governments appear not to make consistent distinctions between investments of foreign nationals and local residents of foreign ethnic stock. Probably the most important reason for the discrepancies in official data is the fact that many investments are simply not reported to governments.

Some countries—Taiwan, for example—require governmental approval of outgoing investments. If ways can be found to take the funds out without reporting the investment, that route may be followed. Indian data are probably fairly accurate compared to those of some other countries, but there are omissions. I have encountered an Indian subsidiary in one country that has spawned a subsidiary elsewhere,

Table A.2
Stock of foreign investment from Latin American countries, as reported by host governments

Country of origin	Registered accumulated flows for host countries (× $1,000)									
	Argentina (8/1976)	Bolivia (1976)	Brazil (6/1978)	Colombia (1978)	Chile (8/1978)	Ecuador (1977)	Mexico (1978)	Peru (1977)	Venezuela (1978)	Total
Argentina		441	20,031	1,062	662	10,876	986	1,771	2,058	37,851
Bolivia	2,605		17	5	133			431	49	3,246
Brazil	16,899	1,301		2,404	13,969	4,752	734	949	338	41,336
Colombia	22,043		244		56	10,347		695	1,499	34,876
Chile	355	271	273	195		11,097	218	1,240	82	13,731
Ecuador			148	17,620	100			825	21	18,714
Mexico	762		7,650	4,142	2,552	4,771		1,156	1,846	22,879
Paraguay			1						77	78
Peru	8	594	14	1,719	47	1,186	133		193	3,894
Uruguay	7,930		16,475	1,110	300			2,256	3,816	31,884
Venezuela	10,090		13,333	26,123	5,697	5,525	1,205	2,011		63,989
Other Latin American countries			194	278	82			38	731	1,323
Total	60,682	2,607	58,380	54,659	23,592	48,524	3,276	11,372	10,706	273,798

Source: Calculated from official sources. For details, see Eduardo White, "The International Projection of Firms from Latin American Countries," in Krishna Kumar and Maxwell McLeod, eds., *Multinationals from Developing Countries* (Lexington, Mass.: Lexington Books, 1981). p. 160.

apparently without the knowledge of the Indian authorities. Moreover, Indian official data do not include all nonmanufacturing investments, even of India's state enterprises. Bharat Heavy Electricals, Ltd., for example, has offices in London and Moscow, "project offices" in New Zealand and Malaysia, and "project coordinating groups" in Libya and Saudi Arabia.[4] These investments, no doubt small and legal, go unreported in official data. For some other countries, many unreported projects were identified. We uncovered quite a few foreign manufacturing (and other) projects of Peruvian firms that were unreported in the official government lists of Peruvian foreign direct investments. India and Peru, like Taiwan, require that their firms obtain government approval before investing abroad. Thus, it is not surprising that some Peruvian firms invest abroad without reporting their activities. Paradoxically, those countries that do not require approval for outgoing investment sometimes have no data or inaccurate data on foreign investment by their firms. Mexico and Hong Kong claim not to collect any data on foreign investment by their enterprises.

One might suspect that host country data are more reliable than home country data. This is probably the case. But there are reasons for underreporting to the host government as well. In some Southeast Asian countries, for example, Chinese investors are unpopular. Rather than risk rejection in the approval process for incoming investment, many simply do not register their investment at all. Thus, much Chinese investment in Indonesia from Singapore and Hong Kong is not registered as such.[5] Moreover, in many countries a foreign investor receives less favorable treatment than a domestic investor. As a result, some foreign investors hide their identity. Managers of one firm in Brazil have gone to great lengths to obscure their ties to their parent located in another Latin American country. They pointed out the many advantages, including favored access to the local credit market, that accrue to a firm thought of as being Brazilian. On the other hand, some countries treat foreign investors better than local firms. Interviews suggested that this was the case in Thailand; there the incentive for a foreign investor is to register as such.

Summaries of official data from a number of host governments on stocks of foreign direct investment by home country of the investor are presented for Asia in table A.1 and for Latin America in table A.2. When more detailed data were available from sources other than those used by the United Nations and INTAL, the additional figures are summarized by home country.

Argentina

The Argentine government reported the following authorized outgoing investment for January 1, 1978, through March 31, 1980.[6]

Destination	Investment ($\times$ $1,000)	Number of projects
Peru	20,118	3
Brazil	6,506	11
United States	5,167	3
Chile	4,723	8
Uruguay	3,206	9
Venezuela	2,617	4
Bolivia	2,015	5
Paraguay	1,894	5
Ecuador	1,565	3
Colombia	1,099	2
Panama	810	1
Germany	480	2
Spain	390	2
Mexico	380	1
Italy	350	2
Honduras	216	1
Costa Rica	135	1
Belgium	97	1
France	20	1
Total	51,784	65

From 1967 to 1977, the Argentine government authorized some $11 million of foreign investment.

These figures do not include the very large holdings of Bunge y Born, whose investments began much earlier. According to the report, Argentine firms control more than $400 million of assets in Brazil.[7]

Hong Kong

Hong Kong does not report on outgoing direct investments. The following are data from host governments and other sources.

Destination	Investment ($\times$ $1,000)	Number of projects
Taiwan (1952–1978)[a]	222,900	847
Singapore (1961–1973)[b]	70,000	
Malaysia (through 1977)[c]	114,700	
Indonesia (through 1976)[d]	662,000	120
Thailand (through 1976)[e]	10,900	
Philippines (through 1976)[e]	14,200	
Vietnam (through 1976)[f]	30,000–50,000	

a. Taiwan government data.

b. Reported in Helen Hughes and You Poh Sing, eds., *Foreign Investment and Industrialization in Singapore* (Madison: University of Wisconsin, 1969).

c. Edward K. Y. Chen, "Hong Kong Multinationals in Asia," in Krishna Kumar and Maxwell McLeod, eds., *Multinationals from Developing Countries* (Lexington, Mass.: Lexington Books, 1981).

d. Indonesian government approvals.

e. U.N. Centre on Transnational Corporations.

f. *South China Morning Post*, January 31, 1977, p. 1.

India

The Indian government reports fairly complete information on approved outgoing direct investment. The following summarizes the figures by stage of implementation as of January 31, 1980.

Status of investment	Total investment ($\times$ $1,000)[a]
In production	38,175
Not in production	61,138
Total	99,313

a. Calculated by Raj Aggarwal and James K. Weekly at 8 rupees to one U.S. dollar.

The numbers of projects are reported by destination in official sources. As of January 31, 1980, they were as follows:

Destination	Number of projects
Southeast Asia	79
Africa	39
West Asia	38
Industrialized countries	23
South Asia	13
Total	192

Source: Raj Aggarwal and James K. Weekly, from *Indian and Foreign Review*, April 1, 1980.

Korea

The Bank of Korea reports on outgoing direct investment. Through 1978, they report the following:

Destination	Investment (× $1,000)	Number of projects
Southeast Asia	46,898	66
Middle East	7,500	16
North America	25,294	84
Latin America	1,798	16
Europe	2,934	42
Africa	22,906	16
Oceania	1,858	3
Total	109,188	243[a]

a. Only 19 of the projects ($18,196,000) were for manufacturing.

Singapore

No official Singapore data were uncovered. The following data come from various sources.

Destination	Investment (× $1,000)	Number of projects
Malaysia (through 1977)[a]	216,900	400[e]
Indonesia (through 1976)[b]	154,600	50
Thailand (through 1976)[c]	2,200	
Hong Kong (through 1976)[c]	13,400	
Vietnam (through 1976)[d]	61,000	

a. *Far Eastern Economic Review*, October 19, 1979, p. 8.
b. Indonesian government approvals.
c. U.N. Centre on Transnational Corporations.
d. Christopher Saint, "Singapore Considers Investments in Vietnam," *World Star*, August 15, 1977.
e. Industrial projects.

Taiwan

The Investment Commission, Ministry of Economic Affairs, reports on outgoing direct investment. From 1959–1978, they report the following:

Destination	Investment ($\times$ $1,000)	Number of projects
Thailand	4,664	22
Malaysia	2,112	18
Singapore	4,002	14
Philippines	9,863	8
Indonesia[a]	5,135	8
United States	8,216	14
Others	15,904	40
Total	49,896	124

a. Through 1976, the Indonesian government reports approvals of $106 million.

Notes

Chapter 1

1. Book value of equity and long-term debt held in foreign subsidiaries of U.S. parents in 1969. Raymond Vernon, *Sovereignty at Bay* (New York: Basic Books, 1971), p. 18.

2. "Singapore Survey," *The Economist*, December 29, 1979, p. 9.

3. Data from *World Development Report, 1980: Annex: World Development Indicators* (Washington, D.C.: The World Bank, August 1981).

4. For a summary of literature, see Louis T. Wells, Jr., and Pankaj Ghemawat, "The Generation of Industrial Technology by the Less-Developed Countries," mimeograph, Harvard Business School, Boston, August 15, 1980. Particularly revealing are the following: Jorge Katz, "The Creation of Technology in the Argentine Manufacturing Sector," IDB/ECLA Working Paper No. 1, Buenos Aires, 1978; John Fei, "Technology in a Developing Country: The Case of Taiwan," Yale University Economic Growth Center, New Haven, November 1977. See also Diana Crane, "Technological Innovation in Developing Countries: A Review of the Literature," *Research Policy*, September 1977, pp. 374–395.

5. *Indonesia: Investment Opportunities*, Investment Coordinating Board, Jakarta, February 1979, p. 54.

6. In addition to the data reported in this study, see UNCTAD, "Joint Enterprises in Developing Asian, Arab and African Regions," mimeograph, prepared for International Meeting of Latin American Joint Enterprises and Investments, Medellin, July 13–15, 1977.

7. For a study of the politics of Indian policies toward the foreign activities of Indian firms, see Dennis Encarnation, *A Rationalist Theory of Collective Action and the Policy Process: The Political Economy of Capital-State Relations in India*, doctoral dissertation, Duke University, 1982.

8. See Ram Gopal Agrawal, "Joint Ventures Among Developing Asian Countries," UNCTAD TC/B/AC.19/3, 1975; Antonio Casas-González, "Joint Ventures among Latin American Countries, UNCTAD TD/B/AC.19/R.2, October

22, 1975; Pius J. Okigbo, "Joint Ventures Among African Countries," UNCTAD TD/B/AC.19/R.3, October 2, 1975; and Ibrahim F. I. Shihata, "Joint Ventures Among Arab Countries," UNCTAD TD/B/AC.19/R.3, October 1975.

9. See Marjan Svetličič, "Strategy and Potentials for Establishing Multinational Enterprises of Developing Countries." Presented at International Workshop on the Promotion of Economic and Technical Co-operation among Developing Countries, Bled, Yugoslavia, November 2–7, 1981 (Research Centre for Co-operation with Developing Countries, Ljubljana, Yugoslavia); Zoran Trputec, "The Rationale for Developing Countries' Joint Ventures." Presented at International Workshop on the Promotion of Economic and Technical Co-operation among Developing Countries, Bled, Yugoslavia, November 2–7, 1981 (Research Centre for Co-operation with Developing Countries, Ljubljana, Yugoslavia); and Louis T. Wells, Jr., "Technology and Third World Multinationals," The MULTI Working Paper Series, International Labour Office, Geneva, 1982.

10. See Peter O'Brien, "The Argentinian Experience in Export of Technology: Retrospect and Prospect," mimeograph, UNIDO, Vienna, 1981; Peter O'Brien et al., "Direct Foreign Investment and Technology Exports among Developing Countries: An Empirical Analysis of the Prospects for Third World Co-operation." Paper for the UNIDO Joint Study on International Industrial Co-operation, Vienna, January 1979; Peter O'Brien and Jan Monkiewicz, "Technology Exports from Developing Countries: The Cases of Argentina and Portugal," UNIDO, Vienna, 1981, UNIDO/IS.218.

11. See, for example, Svetličič, "Strategy and Potentials for Establishing Multinational Enterprises of Developing Countries."

12. See Eduardo White, Jaime Campos, and Guillermo Ondarts, Las Empresas Conjuntas Latinoamericanas (Buenos Aires: Instituto para la Integración de America Latina, 1977).

13. The emphasis on an ownership tie to a parent firm differentiates the firms in this study from the mixture of enterprises discussed in David A. Heenan and Warren J. Keegan, "The Rise of Third World Multinationals," Harvard Business Review, January–February 1979, pp. 101–109.

14. For an argument that significant direct investment from the OPEC countries is likely to occur only when the potential investor faces conditions similar to those discussed in this book, see Stephen J. Kobrin and Donald R. Lessard, "Large Scale Direct OPEC Investment in Industrialized Countries and the Theory of Foreign Direct Investments—A Contradiction?" Weltwirtschaftliches Archiv, Band 112, Heft 4, 1976, pp. 660–673. The efforts of the Investments and Servicing and Promotion Unit of the Arab Fund for Economic and Social Development to place private Arab money in direct investments overseas are discussed in "Let Us Do It for You," The Economist, November 19, 1977, p. 62.

15. For the activities of some of these firms, see J. Panglaykim, Emerging Enterprises in the Asia-Pacific Region (Jakarta: CSIS, 1979), pp. 36–44.

16. We also do not include the firms that have switched from developing country to industrialized country bases, such as the ex-Bolivian Patiño group.

17. For its history, in brief, and its holdings, see Panglaykim, *Emerging Enterprises in the Asia-Pacific Region.*

18. Consistent with its reputation for secrecy, Bunge y Born provided no information for this study. Sketchy data came from articles and the annual reports of one of its foreign affiliates.

19. For a report on investment from the People's Republic of China, see "China's Investments Grow and the Vibes are Good," *Far Eastern Economic Review*, October 6, 1978, pp. 50–60. The so-called multinationals from Russia are covered in Phillip Hill, "The Long Aim of Comecon Multis," *Vision*, February 1977, pp. 45–48. For interesting papers on Spanish foreign investment, see Jose Luis Moreno Mole, "Quince Años de Inversiones Españolas en el Extranjero," and Sebastian de Erice, "Comentarios al Régimen Legal de las Inversiones Españolas en el Extranjero," *Información Comercial Española*, March 1975, pp. 77–89 and pp. 91–107, respectively; and Fernando Varela Parache, "Las Inversiones Españolas en el Extranjero," *Economía Industrial*, August 1972, pp. 59–64.

20. A few qualifying firms might have escaped notice. Identifying international business systems based in developing countries is difficult because of the frequency with which foreign affiliates are held directly by the owners of the "parent firm" or by other affiliates in the home country, rather than by the parent firm itself.

21. Some of the reasons for the discrepancies are discussed in the appendix.

22. Both figures were significant at the .05 level or better.

23. For the summary report on INTAL's work, see Eduardo White, Jaime Campos, and Guillermo Ondarts, *Las Empresas Conjuntas Latinoamericanas* (Buenos Aires: Instituto para la Integración de America Latina, 1977).

Chapter 2

1. Charles P. Kindleberger, *American Business Abroad: Six Lectures on Direct Investment* (New Haven: Yale University Press, 1969), p. 13.

2. See John H. Dunning, "Trade, Location of Economic Activities and the MNE: A Search for an Eclectic Approach," in B. Ohlin, P. O. Hesselborn, and P. M. Wijkman, eds., *The International Allocation of Economic Activity* (New York: Holmes and Meier, 1977).

3. See, for example, Herbert G. Grubel, "Internationally Diversified Portfolios: Welfare Gain and Capital Flows," *American Economic Review*, December 1968, pp. 1299–1314; and John S. Hughes et al., "Corporate International Diversification and Market Assigned Measures of Risk and Diversification," *Journal of Financial and Quantitative Analysis*, November 1975, pp. 627–638.

4. See, for example, Guy V. G. Stevens, "Capital Mobility and the International Firm," in F. Machlup, W. S. Salant, and L. Tarshis, eds., *International Mobility and Movement of Capital* (New York: National Bureau of Economic Research,

1972); Sung Y. Kwack, "A Model of U.S. Direct Investment Abroad: A Neoclassical Approach," *Western Economic Journal*, December 1972, pp. 376–383; and David J. Goldsborough, "The Role of Foreign Direct Investment in the External Adjustment Process," *IMF Staff Papers*, December 1979, pp. 725–754. For a still different approach, but largely within a neoclassical framework, see Robert Z. Aliber, "A Theory of Direct Foreign Investment," in Charles P. Kindleberger, ed., *The International Corporation* (Cambridge, Mass.: MIT Press, 1970).

5. This important idea is often credited to Stephen H. Hymer's 1960 doctoral dissertation at MIT, later published as *The International Operations of National Firms: A Study of Direct Foreign Investment* (Cambridge, Mass.: MIT Press, 1976). For work drawing on the idea, see, for example, Richard E. Caves, "International Corporations: The Industrial Economics of Foreign Investment," *Economica*, February 1971, pp. 1–27; Richard E. Caves, "Causes of Direct Investment: Foreign Firms' Shares in Canadian and United Kingdom Manufacturing Industries," *Review of Economics and Statistics*, August 1974, pp. 279–293; John H. Dunning, "Explaining Changing Patterns of International Production: In Defense of the Eclectic Theory," *Oxford Bulletin of Economics and Statistics* 41 (1979), pp. 269–296; and C. Frederick Bergsten, T. O. Horst, and T. Moran, *American Multinationals and American Interests* (Washington, D.C.: Brookings Institution, 1978).

6. This theme has been particularly dominant in the work of those associated with Harvard Business School's Multinational Enterprise Project. See, for example, Raymond Vernon, *Sovereignty at Bay* (New York: Basic Books, 1971), chapter 3; and Lawrence Franko, *The European Multinationals* (Stamford, Conn.: Greylock, 1976), chapter 2.

7. For the link between demand and innovation, see Jacob Schmookler, *Invention and Economic Growth* (Cambridge, Mass.: Harvard University Press, 1966). For a summary of empirical findings, see Richard S. Rosenbloom, "Technological Innovation in Firms and Industries: An Assessment of the State of the Art," in P. Kelly and M. Dranzberg, eds., *Technological Innovation: A Critical Review of Current Knowlege* (San Francisco: San Francisco Press, 1978).

8. For an early article on this theme, see Raymond Vernon, "International Investment and International Trade in the Product Cycle," *Quarterly Journal of Economics*, May 1966, pp. 190–207. For a summary of empirical findings on the trade aspect, see Louis T. Wells, Jr., ed., *The Product Life Cycle and International Trade* (Boston: Division of Research, Harvard Graduate School of Business Administration, 1972).

9. For a fuller description of the patterns in Europe, see Franko, *The European Multinationals*. See also William H. Davidson, "Patterns of Factor-saving Innovation in the Industrialized World," *European Economic Review* 8 (1976), p. 214.

10. Franko, *The European Multinationals*, pp. 34–44.

11. For an interesting example, consider the use of thin saw blades to cut logs. "Logging Across the Ocean," *The Economist*, May 24, 1980, p. 43. For fuller

descriptions, see Yoshi Tsurumi, *The Japanese Are Coming* (Cambridge, Mass.: Ballinger Publishing Co., 1976); and M. Y. Yoshino, *The Japanese Multinational Enterprise* (Cambridge, Mass.: Harvard University Press, 1977). For different views, see K. Kujima, *Direct Foreign Investment: A Japanese Model of Multinational Business Operations* (London: Croom Helm, 1978).

12. See, for example, Raymond Vernon, "Gone Are the Cash Cows of Yesteryear," *Harvard Business Review*, November–December 1980, pp. 150–163. The weakening of the technology gap and product cycle models of trade from which these ideas have evolved has not necessarily meant a return to neoclassical theories of trade based on factor endowments. Paul Krugman (see, for example, his "Intraindustry Specialization and the Gains from Trade," *Journal of Political Economy*, October 1981) and others have returned to ideas set forth by Staffan Burenstam Linder more than two decades ago (see *An Essay on Trade and Transformation* [Stockholm: Almqvist & Wiksells, 1961]). Rather than expecting the most intensive trade between countries with the greatest differences in factor endowments, some economists are emphasizing theories that predict intensive trade between countries with similar markets and, as a rule, with similar factor endowments.

13. See also Louis T. Wells, Jr., and Pankaj Ghemawat, "The Generation of Industrial Technology Among the Developing Countries," mimeograph, Council on Science and Technology, August 15, 1980.

14. For evidence on this point, see the extensive references in footnotes 11 and 12 of chapter 3 and the footnotes in table 3–5 in Vernon, *Sovereignty at Bay*.

15. Dunning, "Trade, Location of Economic Activities and the MNE"; Peter J. Buckley and Mark Casson, *The Future of the Multinational Enterprise* (London: Macmillan, 1976); Mark Casson, *Alternatives to the Multinational Enterprise* (London, MacMillan, 1979). Much of the work on internalization and international business derives from the ideas of R. H. Coase, "The Nature of the Firm," *Economica N.S.*, no. 4 (1937), pp. 386–405. Reprinted in G. J. Stigler and K. E. Boulding, eds., *Readings in Price Theory* (Homewood, Ill.: Richard D. Irwin, Inc., 1952); Oliver E. Williamson, *Marketing and Hierarchies: Analysis and Antitrust Implications* (New York: Free Press, 1975); and Kenneth J. Arrow, *Limits of Organization* (New York: W. W. Norton, 1974).

Chapter 3

1. P. T. Sirisena, "An Evaluation of the Efficiency, Foreign Exchange Savings and the Welfare Impact of the Steel Industry in Sri Lanka," *Staff Studies* 5 (September 1975), pp. 15–32. For evidence that the socialist suppliers provided technology of a scale similar to that of capitalist suppliers, see UNCTAD, "Major Issues Arising from the Transfer of Technology: A Case Study of Sri Lanka," TD/B/C.6/6, 35, October 7, 1975.

2. For a summary of approaches to down-scaling, see R. B. McKern, "Working Paper," for Experts Meeting on Down-scaling and Adaptation of Industrial Technology, Paris, OECD, June 27–29, 1977.

3. These and other results are reported in Donald Lecraw, "Direct Investment by Firms from Less Developed Countries," *Oxford Economic Papers*, November 1977, pp. 442–457.

4. Donald Lecraw, "The Internationalization of Firms from LDC's: evidence from the ASEAN Region," in Krishna Kumar and Maxwell McLeod, eds., *Multinationals from Developing Countries* (Lexington, Mass.: Lexington Books, 1981).

5. Yung W. Rhee and Larry E. Westphal, "A Note on Exports of Technology from the Republics of China and Korea," mimeograph, 1978, p. 10.

6. See 1973 annual report of Santista Textiles.

7. The two largest weaving factories and the two largest spinning facilities of the Hong Kong firms belonged to "Textile Alliance, Ltd." a firm 45 percent owned by Toray of Japan and highly integrated into the international network of that parent. Because of its ownership, Textile Alliance was included in the study with some hesitancy.

8. See 1973 annual report of Santista Textiles.

9. Lest the reader conclude from these figures that Hong Kong firms are especially large, the average annual sales for different groups of firms were compared, where data were available. The figures for Hong Kong firms were smaller than those for Argentine firms. The average Hong Kong firm is almost exactly the same size as the average foreign investor from all developing countries.

10. C. N. S. Nambudiri et al., in Kumar and McLeod, eds., *Multinationals from Developing Countries*. The study did not clearly distinguish operations owned by foreign firms from operations owned by entrepreneurs of foreign ethnic stock.

11. Louis T. Wells, Jr., "Economic Man and Engineering Man," *Public Policy*, Summer 1973, pp. 319–342.

12. For a number of examples of small-scale technologies that have generated foreign investment in Latin America, see Eduardo White, "The International Projection of Firms from Latin American Countries," in Kumar and McLeod, eds., *Multinationals from Developing Countries*.

13. C. G. Baron, "Sugar Processing Techniques in India," mimeograph from International Labour Office, Geneva, January 1973; and M. K. Garg, "The Scaling-Power of Modern Technology: Crystal Sugar Manufacturing in India," in Nicolas Jequier, ed., *Appropriate Technology Problems and Promises* (Paris: Development Centre of the OECD, 1976). In the case of sugar, the small-scale technology uses more sugar cane.

14. UNCTAD, "Major Issues Arising from the Transfer of Technology," table 13 presents comparable data for a few firms in Sri Lanka. The developing country investors are the most labor-intensive of the group.

15. See Donald Lecraw, "Choice of Technology in Low-Wage Countries: The Case of Thailand," doctoral dissertation in business economics, Harvard Uni-

versity, 1976; and Donald Lecraw, "Direct Investment by Firms from Less Developed Countries."

16. See Ashok Desai, "Research and Development in India," *Margin*, January 1975, p. 90.

17. Note that in many poorer countries, machinery may be imported with little or no duty, while final products face heavy import barriers.

18. See Nathan Rosenberg, Alexander Thompson, and Steven E. Belsley, "Technology Change and Productivity in the Air Transport Industry," NASA *Technical Memorandum 78505*, Moffett Field, Calif., September 1978; Nathan Rosenberg, "Learning by Using," mimeograph, Stanford University, n.d. See also Henry J. Bruton, "On the Production of Appropriate Technology," Research Memorandum Series, No. 13, The Center for Development Economics, Williams College, December 1979, pp. 42–48; and Eric von Hippel, "Users as Innovators," *Technology Review*, January 1978, pp. 31–39.

19. Wen-Lee Ting and Chi Schive, "Direct Investment and Technology Transfer from Taiwan," in Kumar and McLeod, eds., *Multinationals from Developing Countries*.

20. The relation of scale to used equipment is explored in Dilmus James, "Used Automated Plants in Less Developed Countries: A Case Study of a Mexican Firm," *Interamerican Economic Affairs*, vol. 27, no. 1, Summer 1973.

21. The characteristics of second-hand machinery are complex. An interesting study of second-hand jute processing equipment points out that such equipment appears on the market at various times for a number of reasons: changes may occur in machinery technology, product demand may shift, maintenance costs may become too high for a high-wage country, and so on. See Charles Cooper and Raphael Kaplinsky, "Second-hand Equipment in a Developing Country: Jute Processing in Kenya," Discussion Paper No. 37, Institute for Development Studies, University of Sussex, December 1973. See also Howard Pack, "The Optimality of Used Equipment: Calculations for the Cotton Textile Industry," *Economic Development and Cultural Change*, January 1978, pp. 307–324.

22. See R. B. McKern, Working Paper for the OECD Development Centre Experts Meeting on Down-Scaling and Adaptation of Industrial Technology, Paris, April 1977.

23. Edward K. Y. Chen, "Hong Kong Multinationals in Asia," in Kumar and McLeod, eds., *Multinationals from Developing Countries*.

24. Marion R. Foote, "Controlling the Cost of International Compensation," *Harvard Business Review*, November–December 1977, p. 124. See also Nambudiri et al., "Third World Investors in Nigeria," in Kumar and McLeod, eds., *Multinationals from Developing Countries*.

25. See, for example, R. Hal Mason, "The Transfer of Technology and the Factor Proportions Problem: The Philippines and Mexico," *UNITAR Research Report No. 10*, U.N. Institute for Training and Research, New York, n.d.

26. The operation is a Japanese investment operating under U.S. license.

27. Reported in Vinod Busjeet, "Foreign Investors from Less-Developed Countries: A Strategic Profile," unpublished doctoral dissertation, Harvard Business School, 1980.

28. See Donald Lecraw, "Choice of Technology in Low-Wage Countries: The Case of Thailand," unpublished doctoral dissertation in business economics, Harvard University, 1976.

29. See, for example, Cooper and Kaplinsky, "Second-hand Equipment in a Developing Country."

30. See the description in R. B. McKern, Working Paper for the OECD Development Centre Experts Meeting on Down-Scaling and Adaptation of Industrial Technology, pp. 29–35. See also Thomas G. Parry, "The Multinational Enterprise and Two-Stage Technology Transfer to Developing Countries," in Robert G. Hawkins and A. J. Prasad, eds., *Research in International Business and Finance* (Greenwich, Conn.: JAI Press, Inc., 1981), vol. 2, pp. 175–192.

31. For a brief description, see Jorge Casta Castaneda, "La Exportación de Capitales como Inversión," *Uno Mas Uno*, August 13, 1980.

Chapter 4

1. The extent of the constraints posed by Indian import controls is pointed out in Mark Frankena, "Devaluation, Recession, and Nontraditional Manufactured Exports from India," *Economic Development and Cultural Change*, October 1975, pp. 109–137.

2. Ashok Desai, "Research and Development in India," *Margin*, January 1975, p. 79.

3. See "Packages Limited," Intercollegiate Case Clearing House, Boston, Case 9–381–027, 1980.

4. Interestingly, in the seventeenth and eighteenth centuries, it was the United States that remained with charcoal for iron reduction, while Britain, short of wood, moved on to coke.

5. Data collected by Donald Lecraw.

6. There are various examples of such innovations, such as W. R. Grace's use of bagasse for paper making in Peru (an operation subsequently sold by Grace).

7. For evidence of similar behavior with respect to technology choice, see Louis T. Wells, Jr., "Economic Man and Engineering Man: Choice of Technology in a Low Wage Country," *Public Policy*, Summer 1973.

8. Transfer prices are those at which the firm transfers goods or services from one affiliate to another.

9. See *Joint Ventures Abroad* (New Delhi: Indian Investment Centre, 1976), pp. 98–99.

10. A drink believed to have curative powers.

11. See G. William Skinner, *Chinese Society in Thailand: An Analytical History* (Ithaca: Cornell University Press, 1957), p. 104.

12. Jorge Katz and Eduardo Ablin, "From Infant Industry to Technology Exports: The Argentine Experience in the International Sale of Industrial Plants and Engineering Works," Working Paper No. 14, IDB/ECLA Research Program, U.N. Commission on Latin America, October 1978, p. 10.

13. See Interbras, *Relatório de Atividades/1978*, p. 11.

14. Warren Hoge, "Brazil Car Maker Finds a Niche," *The New York Times,* September 9, 1980, pp. D1, D14.

15. Little research has been done to shed light on the characteristics of small firms that invest abroad from the advanced countries. See, however, Gerald D. Newbould, Peter J. Buckley, and Jane C. Thurwell, *Going International: The Experience of Smaller Companies Overseas* (New York: John Wiley & Sons, 1978).

Chapter 5

1. Kunio Yoshihara, *Foreign Investment and Domestic Response: Study of Singapore's Industrialization* (Singapore: Eastern University Press, 1976), p. 188.

2. See Louis T. Wells, Jr., "Economic Man and Engineering Man," *Public Policy*, Summer 1973, pp. 319–342.

3. There are other examples of soft drinks developed to local tastes. Some offer prospects for foreign investment. For example, a Brazilian firm, Brahma, opened a soft drink plant in Nigeria in 1980–1981 to produce a typically Brazilian type of soft drink, guarana. See *Tendência's* July 1980 (pp. 36–38) report on Cotia Comércio Exportação e Importação S.A. and Bank of Boston's advertisement in the *Wall Street Journal*, April 22, 1981.

4. Statement by K. Balakrishnan, 11th Alumni Conference, Indian Institute of Management, Ahmadabad, March 28, 1976.

5. The economics are explained in "The Central American Paint Market (A)," a case written by Ralph Z. Sorenson for INCAE, a business school in Nicaragua.

6. In addition to Stelux's annual reports, see "An End to the Comprador Mentality," *Time*, June 27, 1977, p. 13. I encountered a couple of cases in which a developing country firm acquired a financially weak company in Europe or the United States for its technology.

7. Thomas C. Cochran and Ruben E. Reina, *Capitalism in Argentine Culture: A Study of Torcuatu di Tella and S.I.A.M.* (Philadelphia: University of Pennsylvania, 1962), pp. 112–118.

8. Firms do not seem to find the gains from producing in other developing countries substantial enough to offset the transport and duty costs involved in bringing the products back home. An exception was a venture in Spain estab-

lished by Paidos, of Argentina, to have printing done for books that would be sold largely in Argentina. That example seems to have been the result of the especially high value of the Argentine peso in the later 1970s and the few import restrictions imposed by Argentina at the time.

9. See David Morawetz, "Why the Emperor's New Clothes Are Not Made in Colombia," World Bank Staff Working Paper No. 368, January 1980, p. 139.

10. Gary Pursell and Yung Whee Rhee, "A Firm-Level Study of Korean Exports: Marketing Exports," Research Report No. 5, mimeograph from the World Bank.

11. Mark Frankena, "Marketing Characteristics and Prices of Exports of Engineering Goods from India," *Oxford Economic Papers*, March 1973, pp. 127–132.

12. Donald J. Lecraw, "The Internationalization of Firms from LDCs: Evidence from the ASEAN Region," in Krishna Kumar and Maxwell McLeod, eds., *Multinationals from Developing Countries* (Lexington, Mass.: Lexington Books, 1981).

13. Data collected by Donald Lecraw.

14. Interviews with a member of the Ladjevardi family that controlled the Iranian firm.

15. See L. Wells, "Economic Man and Engineering Man," pp. 330–331; and Ralph Z. Sorenson, "An Analysis of Competition Between Local and International Companies in Two Central American Industries," unpublished doctoral dissertation, Harvard Business School, 1966. For examples from Pakistan, see Khawaja Nasir-ud-Deen, *Marketing in Developing Countries* (Karachi: National Book Foundation, 1976), pp. 21–22, 29–31.

16. See Madhav Kacker, *Marketing Adaptation of U.S. Business Firms in India* (New Delhi: S. K. Ghai, Sterling Publishers Pvt. Ltd., 1974), p. 135; and Nathaniel H. Leff, "Multinational Corporate Pricing Strategies in the Developing Countries," *Journal of International Business Studies*, Fall 1975, pp. 55–64.

Chapter 6

1. "Estudio sobre Empresas Conjuntas Latinoamericanas, Informe de Progreso," mimeograph, INTAL, Buenos Aires, 1977, pp. 47–49.

2. "Latin American Joint Enterprises: Summary and Conclusions," mimeograph, chapter VII of Latin American Joint Enterprises, INTAL, presented to the International Meeting on Latin American Joint Enterprises and Investments, Medellin, Colombia, July 13–15, 1977, pp. 3, 6.

3. Donald J. Lecraw, "The Internationalization of Firms from LDCs: Evidence from the ASEAN Region," in Krishna Kumar and Maxwell McLeod, eds., *Multinationals from Developing Countries* (Lexington, Mass.: Lexington Books, 1981).

4. UNCTAD, "Joint Enterprises in Developing Asian, Arab, and African Regions," mimeograph for International Meeting on Latin American Joint Enterprises and Investments, and UNCTAD, "Major Issues Arising from the Transfer

of Technology: A Case Study of Sri Lanka," TD/B/C.6/6, October 7, 1975, p. 50.

5. D. Singh, "Capital Budgeting and Indian Investments in Foreign Countries," *Management International Review*, Issue No. 1, 1977, p. 103. K. Balakrishnan's interviews in India found exports or other business preceding investment in seven out of ten cases. Two of the exceptions were investments in industrialized countries; one of those has since closed. In one further case, a European acquisition was simply the purchase of a plant to be relocated in India.

6. Significant at better than a .01 level.

7. For a review of the effects of these restrictions on Hong Kong investment in Singapore, see Paul Luey, "Hong Kong Investment," in Helen Hughes and You Poh Sing, eds., *Foreign Investment and Industrialization in Singapore* (Madison: University of Wisconsin, 1969), chapter 5; and Kunio Yoshihara, *Foreign Investment and Domestic Response: A Study of Singapore's Industrialization* (Singapore: Eastern University Press, 1976), chapter 7. For a history of restrictions, see Donald B. Keesing and Martin Wolf, *Textile Quotas Against Developing Countries* (London: Trade Policy Research Centre, 1980), chapters 2 and 3. Restraints on Japanese exports have led to similar overseas investments by Japanese firms.

8. Mauritius was one of a group of Asian, Caribbean, and Pacific countries granted special access to the EEC for exports, as previous colonies of Common Market nations.

9. "Survey: Foreign Investment in Asia," *The Economist*, June 23, 1979, p. 29.

10. Information from interviews.

11. Peter O'Brien et al., "Direct Foreign Investment and Technology Exports among Developing Countries: An Empirical Analysis of the Prospects for Third World Co-operation," paper for the UNIDO Joint Study on International Industrial Co-operation, Vienna, January 1979, p. 21.

12. Sanjay Lall, "Third World Technology Transfer and Third World Transnational Companies," mimeograph, p. 11.

13. Talk by K. Balakrishnan, 11th Alumni Conference, Indian Institute of Management, Ahmadabad, March 28, 1976.

14. See Paul Luey, "Hong Kong Investment"; and Yoshihara, *Foreign Investment and Domestic Response*.

15. For pre-1970 data, see James Riedel, *The Industrialization of Hong Kong*, (Tubingen: J. R. B. Mohr, 1974).

16. For the importance of Hong Kong firms in the Greater-Colombo Export Zone, see "Survey: Foreign Investment in Asia," *The Economist*, June 23, 1979, p. 29.

17. Yoshihara, *Foreign Investment and Domestic Response*.

18. See Ron Richardson, "Opening an Offshore Drive," *Far Eastern Economic Review*, December 7, 1979.

19. See, for example, Robert B. Stobaugh, *Nine Manufacturing Investments Abroad and Their Impact at Home* (Boston: Harvard Business School, 1976).

20. See, for example, William H. Davidson, *Corporate Experience Factors in International Investment and Licensing Activity*, unpublished doctoral dissertation, Harvard Business School, 1979.

21. Donald Lecraw, "Choice of Technology in Low-Wage Countries: The Case of Thailand." unpublished doctoral dissertation in business economics, Harvard University, 1976. Others have pointed out that ethnic ties play a role in the decisions of multinationals from the advanced countries to invest in particular overseas sites. See Lawrence G. Franko, *The European Multinationals* (Stamford, Conn.: Greylock, 1976), p. 113, for some hints that the large German community in Brazil may have played a role in Volkswagen's decision to invest there. See also, Yair Aharoni, *The Foreign Investment Decision Process* (Boston: Harvard Business School, Division of Research, 1966); and John J. Teeling, *The Evolution of Offshore Investment*, unpublished doctoral dissertation, Harvard Business School, 1975. For the role played by ethnic Japanese of Brazil in the decisions of Japanese multinationals, see Charles H. Smith, III, *The Characteristics of Japanese Technology Transfer to Brazil*, unpublished doctoral dissertation, George Washington University, 1979. For ethnic ties and decisions of foreign banks to locate in California, see Adrian E. H. Tschoegh, *Essays in Foreign Direct Investment in Banking*, unpublished doctoral dissertation, MIT Sloan School, 1980.

22. D. Singh, "Capital Budgeting and Indian Investments in Foreign Countries," p. 102. For more information on Indian communities abroad, see Mohan Ram, "The Heritage of the Raj," *Far Eastern Economic Review*, November 23, 1979, pp. 35–42; and Hugh Tinker, *The Banyan Tree* (Oxford: Oxford University Press, 1977).

23. It is interesting to note that preferences for partners of similar ethnic background are not limited to firms from developing countries. The French, for example, are likely to join with local French in Mauritius.

24. One such "house," the Birla's, accounts for 45 percent of Indian foreign investment, according to Peter O'Brien, "The New Multinationals: Developing Country Firms in International Markets," *Futures*, August 1980, p. 305.

25. Ambrose Y. C. King and David H. K. Leung, "The Chinese Touch in Small Industrial Organizations," mimeograph, The Chinese University of Hong Kong, Social Research Centre, A53–07–1–5, July 1975, p. 19.

26. In addition to King and Leung, "The Chinese Touch," see John L. Espy, "The Strategies of Chinese Industrial Enterprises in Hong Kong." unpublished doctoral dissertation, Harvard Business School, 1970, pp. 168–175; and Michael R. Godley, *The Mandarin-Capitalists from Nanyang* [Southeast Asia], especially the histories of entrepreneurs on pp. 9–28 and chapter 2, which cites many other studies.

27. For an interesting and instructive study of many small Chinese and Indian businesses run by East Asians in the Philippines, see individual Benedict, "Family Firms

and Firm Families: A Comparison of Indian, Chinese and Creole Firms in Seychelles," in Greenfield et al., eds., *Entrepreneurs in Cultural Context* (Albuquerque: University of New Mexico Press, 1979), pp. 305–328. The Creole families described in the study have, in perhaps a greater extreme, the characteristics often attributed to Latin American families.

28. Gerald L. Gold, "Barley, Compadres, and Fiestas: Investment and Confidence in a Mexican Regional Elite," in Greenfield et al., *Entrepreneurs in Cultural Context*, p. 287.

29. Octavio Paz, *The Labyrinth of Solitude: Life and Thought in Mexico* (New York: Grove Press, 1961), pp. 19, 30.

30. See, for example, the difficulties described in Norm Long, "Multiple Enterprise in the Central Highlands of Peru," in Greenfield et al., *Entrepreneurs in Cultural Context*, pp. 123–158.

31. Thomas C. Cochran and Ruben E. Reina, *Capitalism in Argentine Culture: A Study of Torcuatu di Tella and S.I.A.M.* (Philadelphia: University of Pennsylvania, 1966), pp. 119–130.

32. In fact, a number of conglomerate-like investments encountered in this study seemed to be motivated by the desire for diversification. Thus, a Latin American or a Hong Kong family might have real estate interests in the United States and shares in some manufacturing operations in neighboring countries. The know-how would have nothing in common with the family's operations at home. Although technically direct investment in many cases, there was little interest in management and no common strategy beyond diversification.

33. For the effect of these events on investments, see Luey, "Hong Kong Investment."

34. See Pius J. C. Okigbo, "Joint Ventures Among African Countries," UNCTAD TD/B/AC.19/R.3, October 3, 1975, Annex III, p. 2.

35. For similar examples from early European foreign investments, see Franko, *The European Multinationals*, p. 187. For the role of kinfolk in Chinese firms for handling business matters when the owner is distant, see King and Leung, "The Chinese Touch in Small Industrial Organizations"; and Goh Joon Hai, "Some Aspects of the Chinese Business World in Malaysia," *Ekonomic*, December 1962, pp. 84–93.

36. For an analysis of early decisions by U.S. firms, see Aharoni, *The Foreign Investment Decision Process*.

37. See Leonard Bush, "A Comparative Analysis of Regional Trade and Investment Among Developing Countries of Latin America and South and Southeast Asia," unpublished undergraduate honors thesis, Department of Economics, Harvard College, 1981.

Chapter 7

1. For a summary of literature, see Louis T. Wells, Jr., and Pankaj Ghemawat, "Transfer of Industrial Technology among the Developing Countries," mimeo-

graph for the Council on Science and Technology, Harvard Business School, August 15, 1980. See also Franciso Colman Sercovich, "Brazil as a Technology Exporter (Final Report)," InterAmerican Development Bank, April 1981.

2. Maintaining secrecy is probably particularly easy for the small, often family-run enterprises that were typical of the firms in this study. In comparison to the multinationals from the advanced countries, these firms had to inform only a few, well-trusted people about the illegal transaction. This ability to maintain secrecy appeared also in the seemingly high propensity of foreign investors from developing countries to engage in unofficial payments to government officials.

3. Williamson calls the condition "information impactedness." See Oliver E. Williamson, *Markets and Hierarchies* (New York: Free Press, 1975).

4. Charles Cooper and Raphael Kaplinsky, "Second-hand Equipment in a Developing Country: Jute Processing in Kenya," Discussion Paper No. 37, Institute for Development Studies, University of Sussex, December 1973.

5. Peter M. Blau et al., "Technology and Organization in Manufacturing," *Administrative Science Quarterly*, March 1976, pp. 30, 34.

6. Donald J. Lecraw, "The Internationalization of Firms from LDCs: Evidence from the ASEAN Region," in Krishna Kumar and Maxwell McLeod, eds., *Multinationals from Developing Countries* (Lexington, Mass.: Lexington Books, 1981).

7. Data were available for 244 subsidiaries, 191 of which were for manufacturing.

8. Williamson refers to "bounded rationality" as the reason for the failure of market solutions when the number of contingencies is large. See *Markets and Hierarchies*.

9. Williams refers to the problem as "opportunism." Once a transaction is entered, a small numbers problem exists through "first mover" advantages. One party may take advantage of the situation in new negotiations. See *Markets and Hierarchies*. Others have included the same issue under "bilateral monopoly." For an example of the concept applied to Swiss foreign investment, see Jürg Niehans, "Benefits of Multinational Firms from a Small Parent Economy: The Case of Switzerland," in Tamir Agmon and Charles P. Kindleberger, eds., *Multinationals from Small Countries* (Cambridge, Mass.: The MIT Press, 1977), pp. 15–16.

10. Even in this case, one could think of complicated provisions for a contract to compensate the one firm for the costs of trained managers.

11. In fact, this kind of drive for diversification probably partly explains the high propensity of overseas subsidiaries of firms from developing countries to be owned by the parent firms' owners rather than by the firms themselves.

12. For the experience of this and other Brazilian firms, see Sercovich, "Brazil as a Technology Exporter."

13. For many examples, see Sercovich, "Brazil as a Technology Exporter"; Sanjay Lall, "Developing Countries as Exporters of Industrial Technology,"

Research Policy, January 1980, pp. 24–52 (for India); Jorge Katz and Eduardo Ablin, "From Infant Industry to Technology Exports: The Argentine Experience in the International Sale of Industrial Plants and Engineering Works," IDB/ECLA Working Paper Number 14, Buenos Aires, 1978 (for Argentina); and Yung W. Rhee and Larry E. Westphal, "A Note on Exports of Technology from the Republics of China and Korea," mimeograph, 1978, p. 10 (for Taiwan and Korea).

14. That is, 95–100 percent.

15. See, for example, Eduardo White, Jaime Campos, and Guillermo Ondarte, *Las Empresas Conjuntas Latinoamericanas* (Buenos Aires: INTAL, 1977), chapter IV; and the various studies reported in Kumar and McLeod, eds., *Multinationals from Developing Countries.*

16. For a treatment of ownership patterns of U.S. multinationals, see John M. Stopford and Louis T. Wells, Jr., *Managing the Multinational Enterprise* (New York: Basic Books, 1972), chapters 7–12.

17. See Stopford and Wells, *Managing the Multinational Enterprise.*

18. Kunio Yoshihara, *Foreign Investment and Domestic Response: A Study of Singapore's Industrialization* (Singapore: Eastern University Press, 1976), p. 141.

19. Interviews by Carlos Cordeiro.

20. Sung-Hwan Jo, "Overseas Direct Investment by South Korean Firms: Direction and Pattern," in Kumar and McLeod, eds., *Multinationals from Developing Countries.*

21. Stopford and Wells, *Managing the Multinational Enterprise.*

22. For an empirical analysis of the impact of bargaining power on ownership of subsidiaries of U.S. firms in Latin America, see Nathan Fagre and Louis T. Wells, Jr., "Bargaining Power of Multinationals and Host Governments," *Journal of International Business* (forthcoming).

23. See Stopford and Wells, *Managing the Multinational Enterprise,* chapter 9. For a demonstration that similar relationships hold for Japanese firms, see Yoshihara, "Strategy and Ownership."

24. Blau, "Technology and Organization," p. 24.

25. D. R. Singh, "Capital Budgeting and Indian Investments in Foreign Countries," *Management International Review* 17, (1977), p. 103.

26. Paul Luey and Ung Gim Sei, "Taiwan Investment," in Helen Hughes and You Poh Sing, eds., *Foreign Investment and Industrialization in Singapore* (Madison: University of Wisconsin, 1969), pp. 126–127, 143–144.

Chapter 8

1. Hugh Tinker, *The Banyan Tree: Overseas Emigrants from India, Pakistan, and Bangladesh* (Oxford: Oxford University Press, 1977), pp. 3, 143–150.

2. U.S. Department of Commerce, *Foreign Direct Investment in the United States,* Interim Report to Congress, Volume 1, October 1975, VII-16 and VII-17.

3. Representative offices were not included in the Department of Commerce data or in our data.

4. For a test of the relation between trade and banking investments, see Adrian Edward Henry Tschoegl, "Essays in Foreign Direct Investment in Banking," unpublished Ph.D. dissertation, Sloan School, MIT, 1980. For the role of trade in the establishment of European operations by Arab banks, see Paul Leins, "Arab Banks Alive and Well in Paris," *New York Times,* November 26, 1977, p. 1 of business section.

5. Among major financial institutions, the problem of enforcement is probably less serious than for manufacturing firms, given the tendency of transactions to be undertaken based on trust.

6. Sy Cip, Gorres, Velayo and Company from the Philippines.

7. See ad on p. 74, *The Economist,* October 25, 1975.

8. Data reported in Yuan-li Wu and Chun-hsi Wu, *Economic Development in Southeast Asia: The Chinese Dimension* (Stanford, Calif.: Hoover Institution, 1980), p. 99.

9. The Hong Kong-Shanghai Bank was in the process of acquiring a major interest in the U.S. Marine Midland Bank at the time of this writing.

10. In this case, the management is unquestionably Indian. The influence of ethnic Britishers is strong in the Hong Kong cases. For more on international hotels, including those based in developing countries, see John H. Dunning and Matthew McQueen, "The Eclectic Theory of International Production: A Case Study of the International Hotel Industry," University of Reading Discussion Papers in International Investment and Business Studies No. 55, August 1981.

11. *India's Joint Ventures Abroad* (New Delhi: Indian Institute of Foreign Trade, n.d. (1978?)).

12. Christopher Sweeney, "The End of a Building Boom," *Far Eastern Economic Review,* July 25, 1980, p. 38.

13. "Korean Firms Gain Respect as Technology Exporters," *Business Asia,* November 30, 1973, p. 381.

14. Kyung-Il Ghymn, "Multinational Enterprises from Developing Countries: The Experience of Korea," mimeograph, presented at the 1978 meetings of the Academy of International Business.

15. Kyung-Il Ghymn, "Multinational Enterprises from the Third World," mimeograph, presented at the 1980 meetings of the Academy of International Business, p. 5.

16. Reported in Raj Aggarwal and James K. Weekly, "Foreign Operations of Third World Multinationals," mimeograph, presented at the 1980 meetings of the Academy of International Business.

17. "Mað-de-Obra: Lei Discriplinara Salda Para O Exterior," *Comércio y Mercados*, December 1978, p. 37.

18. Kyung-Il Ghymn, "Multinational Enterprises from the Third World."

19. Nigeria has also recruited other professionals from Brazil, such as doctors and architects. See "Mað-de-Obra."

20. "Competing for Third World Contracts," *Brazilian Business*, November 1979, pp. 19–22. For an analysis closely related to that of this section, see "Brazil: Constructivism," *The Economist*, October 27, 1979, p. 80.

21. "Italy's World Builders," *The Economist*, November 11, 1978, p. 81.

22. This seems to be the case with ICA International C.A., a Mexican firm. See Antonio Casas-González, "Joint Ventures among Latin American Countries," UNCTAD TD/B/AC.19/R.2, October 22, 1975, pp. 6–7.

23. See "Italy's World Builders," *The Economist*, November 11, 1978, p. 80.

24. Sung-Hwan Jo, "Overseas Direct Investment by South Korean Firms: Direction and Pattern," in Krishna Kumar and Maxwell McLeod, eds., *Multinationals from Developing Countries* (Lexington, Mass.: Lexington Books, 1981).

25. Ibid.

26. For a description of Korean interest in various coal projects, see Ron Richardson, "South Korea Tries to Buy a Guarantee," *Far Eastern Economic Review*, August 31, 1979, pp. 76–79.

27. See "India Helps the Ayatollah," *The Economist*, June 21, 1980, p. 87.

28. *Braspetro Annual Report*, 1978.

29. Krishna Kumar, "Overseas Direct Investment by Public Sector Enterprises of LDC's," in Kumar and McLeod, eds., *Multinationals from Developing Countries*.

30. Twenty-one state-owned raw material projects were uncovered.

31. Stephen J. Kobrin and Donald R. Lessard, "Large Scale Direct OPEC Investment in Industrialized Countries and the Theory of Foreign Direct Investment—A Contradiction?", *Weltwirtschaftliches Archiv*, Band 112, Heft 4, 1976, p. 669.

32. For the debate in Korea about the merits of direct investment and long-term contracts for coal, see Richardson, "South Korea Tries to Buy a Guarantee."

33. "OPEC's Real Problems," *The Economist*, July 9, 1977, p. 86.

34. L. G. Franko, "Multinational Enterprise: The International Division of Labour in Manufactures, and the Developing Countries," Working Paper of the World Employment Programme Research, International Labour Office, Geneva, October 1975, p. 16.

35. Peter O'Brien et al., "Direct Foreign Investment and Technology Exports among Developing Countries: An Empirical Analysis of the Prospects for Third World Co-operation," paper for the UNIDO Joint Study on International Industrial Co-operation, Vienna, January 1979, p. 25.

36. Raymond Vernon, "Opportunities and Challenges for Multinational Firms from Developing Countries," Seminar Series No. 24, Korea International Economic Institute, August 1979.

Chapter 9

1. Quoted in Dilip Mukerjee, "An Asian Role in Africa," *Far Eastern Economic Review*, July 18, 1980, p. 47.

2. Under the Egyptian Law 43 on Foreign Investment, 1974.

3. For some questions about the actual merits, see chapter 11 of John M. Stopford and Louis T. Wells, Jr., *Managing the Multinational Enterprise* (New York: Basic Books, 1972).

4. Interviews by Donald Lecraw.

5. Donald J. Lecraw, "Internationalization of Firms from LDCs: Evidence from the ASEAN Region," in Krishna Kumar and Maxwell McLeod, eds., *Multinationals from Developing Countries* (Lexington, Mass.: Lexington Books, 1981), p. 84.

6. The merits of such a sector are hotly debated. For some of the arguments against offshore plants, see Folker Frobel, Jurgen Heinrichs, and Otto Kreye, *The New International Division of Labour* (Cambridge: Cambridge University Press, 1980), the English translation of a book published in German in 1977. Recent work suggests that offshore plants may spread special technology in the host country to a greater extent than many critics had suspected. See Mark Lester, "Impact of EPZ's in Developing Countries: Transfer of Managerial and Technological Skills in the Semiconductor Assembly Industry," mimeograph, prepared for second WEPZA General Assembly Meeting, Philippines, March 23–27, 1981.

7. E. F. Schumacher, *Small Is Beautiful* (New York: Harper & Row Publishers, 1973).

8. See Nathan Fagre and Louis T. Wells, Jr., "Bargaining Power of Multinationals and Host Governments," *Journal of International Business Studies* (forthcoming).

9. See Peter Weintraub and B. H. S. Jayewardene, "Singapore Looks Further Afield," *Far Eastern Economic Review*, May 12, 1978, pp. 40–43.

10. For an excellent treatment of Indian policies and Indian politics with respect to overseas investments of Indian firms, see Dennis J. Encarnation, "The Political Economy of Indian Joint Industrial Ventures Abroad: A Study of Domestic Policies and Transnational Linkages," *International Organization* (forthcoming).

11. "Regulation Governing Outward Investment," promulgated by Executive Yuan Order No. 3646 on June 20, 1967, by Executive Yuan Order No. 5531 and on January 19, 1972, by Executive Yuan Order No. 0541.

12. See, for example, Ron Richardson, "South Korea Tries to Buy a Guarantee," *Far Eastern Economic Review*, August 31, 1979, p. 78, for Korea's incentives. See also John Venturos Abroad (New Delhi: Indian Investment Centre, 1976).

13. See, for example, UNIDO, *Industry 2000: New Perspectives*, Third General Conference of UNIDO, New Delhi, January 21–February 8, 1980, Agenda items 4(b) and 5, ID/CONF.4/3, August 30, 1979, chapter 7.

14. For a description of Decision 46 and some proposed integration projects, see Carlos F. Díaz-Alejandro, "Foreign Direct Investment by Latin Americans," in Tamir Agmon and Charles P. Kindleberger, eds., *Multinationals from Small Countries* (Cambridge, Mass.: MIT Press, 1977), pp. 167–196. For SELA, see Robert D. Bond, "Regionalism in Latin America: Prospects for the Latin American Economic System (SELA)," *International Organization*, Spring 1978, pp. 402–423.

15. With exception of the technology source, such enterprises are in many cases quite similar to those developed by governments in Europe for nuclear energy, aircraft, and weapons development.

16. The two cement proposals are described in more detail in Pius N. C. Okigbo, "Joint Ventures among African Countries," UNCTAD TD/B/AC.19/R.3, October 2, 1975, Annex III.

17. Information from interviews, T.A.L. annual reports, and Paul Wilson and Susuma Awanohara, "Faith, Hope and Heavy Losses," *Far Eastern Economic Review*, September 1, 1978, p. 98.

18. A memo presented by the Federation of Indian Chambers of Commerce and Industry to Parliament in 1972 and quoted in Encarnation, "The Political Economy of Indian Joint Industrial Ventures Abroad."

Chapter 10

1. See Robert Stobaugh, "The Oil Companies in the Crisis," *Daedalus*, Fall 1975, pp. 179–202.

Appendix

1. United Nations Economic and Social Council, *Transnational Corporations in World Development: A Re-examination* (New York: United Nations, 1978), Tables III-40 and III-41, pp. 246, 247.

2. Anthony Edwards, *Asian Industrial Expansion* (London: The Financial Times Limited, 1977), p. 42.

3. Investment Commission, Ministry of Economic Affairs, *Statistics on Overseas Chinese and Foreign Investment, Technical Cooperation, Outward Investment* (Taipei: Government of the Republic of China, December 31, 1978), p. 13.

4. From an organization chart compiled by Lynn H. Distelhorst from a 1978 company telephone book.

5. From interviews and Yuan-li Wu and Chun-hsi Wu, *Economic Development in Southeast Asia: The Chinese Dimension* (Stanford, Calif.: Hoover Institution, 1980), p. 69.

6. Comité de Estudio Patrocinado, "Proyección Externa de la Empresa Argentina," Consejo Argentino para las Relaciones Internacionales, Buenos Aires, August 1980.

7. "Inversiones Argentinas en el Exterior," *B.I.E.L.*, October 1978, pp. 1–2.

Bibliography

The following books, articles, dissertations, and papers devote considerable attention to the foreign investments of firms from developing countries.

Agarwal, Ram Gopal. "Joint Ventures as an Instrument of Export Promotion." *Foreign Trade Review*, January–March 1967, pp. 349+.

Agarwal, Ram Gopal. "Joint Ventures Among Developing Asian Countries." UNCTAD TC/B/AC.19/R.7, 1975.

Agarwal, Ram Gopal. "Third-World Joint Ventures: Indian Experience." In Kumar and McLeod, eds., *Multinationals from Developing Countries*. Lexington, Mass.: Lexington Books, 1981.

Aggarwal, Raj, and Inder P. Khera. "Foreign Operations of Third World Multinationals: A Literature Review and Analysis of Indian Companies." *The Journal of Developing Areas* (forthcoming).

Aggarwal, Raj, and James K. Weekly. "Foreign Operations of Third World Multinationals." Paper presented at the 1980 meetings of the Academy of International Business.

Balakrishnan, K. "Indian Joint Ventures Abroad: Geographic and Industry Patterns." *Economic and Political Weekly*, Review of Management, May 1976.

Balakrishnan, K. "MNC's from LDC's: The Case of Indian Joint Ventures Abroad." Mimeograph, Ahmedabad, March 1980.

"Brazil: Constructivism." *The Economist*, October 27, 1979, p. 80.

Busjeet, Vinod. "Foreign Investors from Less Developed Countries." Unpublished doctoral dissertation, Harvard Business School, 1980.

Calderon-Rossell. "A Proposal: Foreign Direct Investment from Developed versus Developing Countries." Mimeograph, Instituto Centroamericano de Administración de Empresas, Managua, 1977.

Campos, Jaime. "La Actuación Internacional de la Pequeña y Mediana Empresa." INTAL, Buenos Aires, 1977.

Campos, Jaime. "Intercambio Empresarial de Recursos Productivos entre Paises Latinoamericanos." INTAL, Buenos Aires, 1980.

Casas-González, Antonio. "Joint Ventures among Latin American Countries." UNCTAD TD/B/AC.19/R.2, October 22, 1975.

Casas-González, Antonio. "Regional Multinational Firms in Latin America." UNCTAD, Division for Trade Expansion and Economic Integration, October 1975.

Chaudry, N. G. "Joint Ventures Abroad." *Indian and Foreign Review*, April 1980, p. 4.

Chen, Edward K. Y. "Hong Kong Multinationals in Asia: Characteristics and Objectives." In Kumar and McLeod, eds., *Multinationals from Developing Countries*. Lexington, Mass.: Lexington Books, 1981.

Cizelj, Boris, et al. "Joint Ventures through Technical Co-operation among Developing Countries and Their Economic Potentials." Research Centre for Co-operation with Developing Countries, Ljubljana, Yugoslavia, 1981.

Cochran, Thomas E., and Ruben E. Reina. *Capitalism in Argentine Culture: A Study of Torcuatu di Tella and S.I.A.M.* Philadelphia: University of Pennsylvania, 1962.

Comité de Estudio Patrocinado (por el Consejo Argentino para las Relaciones Internacionales). *Proyección Externa de la Empresa Argentina*. Consejo Argentino para las Relaciones Internacionales, Buenos Aires, October 1980.

"Competing for Third World Contracts." *Brazilian Business*, November 1979, pp. 19–22.

Cordeiro, Carlos A. "The Internationalization of Indian Firms: A Case for Direct Foreign Investment from a Less Developed Country." Unpublished undergraduate honors thesis, Department of Economics, Harvard College, 1978.

Diamand, Marcelo. "Las Empresas Conjuntas Latinoamericanas: Coincidencias y Conflictos de Intereses." Estudio 16, INTAL, Buenos Aires, 1976.

Díaz-Alejandro, Carlos. "Inversión Extranjera Directa por Latinoamericanos." *Integración Latinoamericana*, July 1976, pp. 4+.

Díaz-Alejandro, Carlos. "Foreign Direct Investment by Latin Americans." In Tamir Agmon and Charles P. Kindleberger, eds., *Multinationals from Small Countries*. Cambridge, Mass.: MIT Press, 1977.

Dundas, Carl W. "Las Empresas Conjuntas en la Comunidad de Caribe." *Integración Latinoamericana*, September 1977, pp. 61+.

Dunning, John H. "Explaining Outward Investment of Developing Countries: In Support of the Eclectic Theory of International Production." In Kumar and McLeod, eds., *Multinationals from Developing Countries*. Lexington, Mass.: Lexington Books, 1981.

Encarnation, Dennis J. "The Political Economy of Indian Joint Industrial Ventures Abroad: A Study of Domestic Policies and Transnational Linkages." *International Organization*, Winter 1982, pp. 31–59.

Ghymn, Kyung-Il. "Multinational Enterprises from Developing Countries: The Experience of Korea." Paper presented at the 1978 meetings of the Academy of International Business. Mimeograph.

Ghymn, Kyung-Il. "Multinational Enterprises from the Third World." Paper presented at the 1980 meetings of the Academy of Intenational Business. Mimeograph.

Green, Reginald H. "Developing Country Multinational Enterprises: Notes Toward an Operational Component of Third World Economic Co-operation." Conference on Economic Cooperation and Trade among Developing Countries, Tunis, April 1977. Mimeograph.

Heenan, David A., and Warren J. Keegan. "The Rise of Third World Multinationals." *Harvard Business Review*, January–February 1979, pp. 101–109.

"Indian Companies as Foreign Investors." *Business Asia*, December 15, 1978, p. 400.

"Indian Multinationals Spring Fresh Drive into Asian Markets," *Business Asia*, December 19, 1980, pp. 404–405.

India's Joint Ventures Abroad. New Delhi: Indian Institute of Foreign Trade, n.d. (1978?).

INTAL. "Estudio Sobre Empresas Conjuntas Latinamericanas, Informe de Progreso." Mimeograph, INTAL, Buenos Aires, 1977.

INTAL. "Latin American Joint Enterprises." Presented to the International Meeting on Latin American Joint Enterprises and Investments, Medellin, Colombia, July 13–15, 1977.

Jo, Sung-Hwan. "Overseas Direct Investment by South Korean Firms: Direction and Pattern." In Kumar and McLeod, eds., *Multinationals from Developing Countries*. Lexington, Mass.: Lexington Books, 1981.

Jo, Sung-Hwan. "Toward a Development Economic Approach to Explaining the LDC's International Production: Theoretical Implications from the South Korean Experience." Mimeograph, n.d. (1982?).

Joint Ventures Abroad. New Delhi: Indian Investment Centre, 1976.

Katz, Jorge, and Eduardo Ablin. "De la Industria Incipiente a la Exportación de Tecnología: La Experiencia Argentina en la Venta Internacional de Plantas Industriales y Obra de Ingenieria." Programa BID/CEPAL de Investigaciones en Temas de Ciencia y Tecnología, Buenos Aires, 1978.

Katz, Jorge, and Eduardo Ablin. "Tecnología y Exportaciones Industriales: un Analisis Microeconómico de la Experiencia Argentina Reciente." Programa BID/CEPAL de Investigaciones en Temas de Ciencia y Tecnología, Buenos Aires, December 1976.

"Korean Firms Gain Respect as Technology Exporters." *Business Asia*, November 30, 1973, p. 381.

Kumar, Krishna. "Foreign Direct Investment by Korean Firms in Manufacturing Sector." *Asian Finance* (forthcoming).

Kumar, Krishna. "The Korean Manufacturing Multinationals." Mimeograph, Culture Learning Institute, East-West Center, Honolulu, n.d. (1980 or 1981).

Kumar, Krishna. "Multinationalization of Third-World Public-Sector Enterprises." In Kumar and McLeod, eds., *Multinationals from Developing Countries.* Lexington, Mass.: Lexington Books, 1981.

Kumar, Krishna. "Third World Multinationals: A Growing Force in International Relations." *International Studies Quarterly* 26 (September 1982): pp. 397–424.

Kumar, Krishna, and Kee Young Kim. "The Multinationalization of Firms from the Republic of Korea: A Study of the Overseas Investments in the Manufacturing Sector." Mimeograph, 1981.

Lall, Sanjaya. "Developing Countries as Exporters of Industrial Technology." *Research Policy,* January 1980, pp. 24–52.

Lall, Sanjaya. "Developing Countries as Exporters of Technology." In H. Giersch, ed., *International Economic Development and Resource Transfer.* Tubingen: J. C. B. Mohr, 1979.

Lall, Sanjaya. "The Export of Capital from Developing Countries: India." In John Dunning and J. Black, eds., *International Investment and Capital Movements.* London: Macmillan, forthcoming.

Lall, Sanjaya. "Third World Multinationals: A Brief Survey of Theory and Evidence." Mimeograph, Oxford University Institute of Economics and Statistics, Oxford, September 1981.

Lall, Sanjaya. "Third World Technology Transfer and Third World Transnational Companies." Mimeograph.

Lecraw, Donald. "Choice of Technology in Low-Wage Countries." Unpublished doctoral dissertation in business economics, Harvard University, 1976.

Lecraw, Donald. "Direct Investment by Firms from Less Developed Countries." *Oxford Economic Papers,* November 1977, p. 442–457.

Lecraw, Donald. "Internationalization of Firms from LDC's: Evidence from the ASEAN Region." In Kumar and McLeod, eds. *Multinationals from Developing Countries.* Lexington, Mass.: Lexington Books, 1981.

Lecraw, Donald. "Intra-Asian Direct Investment: Theory and Evidence from the ASEAN Region." *UMBC Economic Review,* No. 2, 1980.

Lecraw, Donald. "Structural and Competitive Practices of Transnational Corporations in the ASEAN Region." U.N. Centre on Transnational Corporations, New York, 1979.

Lecraw, Donald. "Technological Activities of LDC-Based Multinationals." *The Annals of the American Academy of Political and Social Sciences,* November 1981.

Lecraw, Donald. "Strategic Groups and the Performance of Transnational Corporations in Less Developed Countries." *Journal of International Business Studies* (forthcoming).

Luey, Paul. "Hong Kong Investment." In Helen Hughes and You Poh Sing, eds., *Foreign Investment and Industrialization in Singapore*. Madison: University of Wisconsin, 1969.

Luey, Paul, and Ung Gim Sei. "Taiwan Investment." In Hughes and You, eds., *Foreign Investment and Industrialization in Singapore*. Madison: University of Wisconsin, 1969.

"Maõ-de-Obra: Lei Discriplinara Salda Para O Exterior." *Comércio y Mercados*, December 1978, pp. 34–37.

Nambudiri, C. D. S., Olukunle Iyandi, and D. M. Akinnus. "Third-World-Country Firms in Nigeria." In Kumar and McLeod, eds., *Multinationals from Developing Countries*. Lexington, Mass.: Lexington Books, 1981.

"The New Multinationals." *Business India*, August 20, 1979, pp. 33–35, and September 2, 1979, pp. 44–47.

Nugent, Jeffrey B. "Multinational Joint Venture Companies of Developing Countries as Instruments of Economic Integration in Development (with Special Reference to the Arab Countries' Experience)." Paper presented at International Workshop on the Promotion of Economic and Technical Cooperation among Developing Countries, Bled, Yugoslavia, November 2–7, 1981. Ljubljana, Yugoslavia: Resource Centre for Co-operation with Developing Countries.

O'Brien, Peter. "The Argentinian Experience in Export of Technology: Retrospect and Prospect." Mimeograph, UNIDO, Vienna, 1981.

OBrien, Peter. "Has Knowledge Trickled Down? The Nature and Implications of the International Projection of Developing Country Firms." *Vierteljahresberichte der Entwicklungsländerforschung*. Special issue on Trends in International Transfer of Technology, March 1981.

O'Brien, Peter. "The Internationalisation of Third World Industrial Firms." *Multinational Business*, no. 4 (1980): pp. 1–8.

O'Brien, Peter. "The New Multinationals: Developing Country Firms in International Markets." *Futures*, August 1980, pp. 303–316.

O'Brien, Peter. "Third World Industrial Enterprises: Export of Technology and Investment." *Economic and Political Weekly*, Special Number, October 1980.

O'Brien, Peter, et al. "Direct Foreign Investment and Technology Exports among Developing Countries: An Empirical Analysis of the Prospects for Third World Co-operation." Paper for the UNIDO Joint Study on International Industrial Co-operation, Vienna, January 1979.

O'Brien, Peter, and Jan Monkiewicz. "Technology Exports from Developing Countries: The Cases of Argentina and Portugal." UNIDO/IS.218, Vienna, 1981.

Okibgo, Pius J. C. "Joint Ventures Among African Countries." UNCTAD TD/B/AC.19/R.3, October 2, 1975.

Panglaykim, J. *Emerging Enterprises in the Asia-Pacific Region*. Jakarta: CSIS, 1979.

Prasad, A. J. "Export of Technology from India." Mimeograph, Columbia University, New York, March 1976.

Raju, M. K. *Internationalization of Indian Business*. Bombay: Forum of Free Enterprise, 1980.

Raju, M. K., and C. K. Prahalad. *The Emerging Multinationals—Indian Experience in the ASEAN Region*. Madras: M. K. Raju Consultants Private Ltd., 1982.

Report of Workshop on Indian Industrial Joint Ventures Abroad. Federation of Indian Chambers of Commerce and Industry, New Delhi, January 23, 1976.

Richardson, Ron. "South Korea Tries to Buy a Guarantee." *Far Eastern Economic Review*, August 31, 1979, pp. 76–79.

Scheman, Ronald L. "The Multinational in a New Mode: Ownership by the Developing Countries." *International Development Review*, vol. 15, no. 2 (1973), pp. 22–24.

Sercovich, Francisco Colman. "Brazil as a Technology Exporter (Final Report)." Mimeograph, Interamerican Development Bank, August 1981.

Shihata, Ibrahim F. I. "Joint Ventures among Arab Countries." UNCTAD, TD/B/AD.19/R.5, October 1975.

Singh, D. "Capital Budgeting and Indian Investments in Foreign Countries." *Management International Review*, Issue No. 1, 1977.

Singh, Harbans. "Prospects of Joint Ventures." Special section on investment opportunities in Sri Lanka in *The Economic Times* (of India), August 13, 1981, pp. IV–V.

Svetličič, Marjan. "Strategy and Potentials for Establishing Multinational Enterprises of Developing Countries." Paper presented at International Workshop on the Promotion of Economic and Technical Co-operation among Developing Countries, Bled, Yugoslavia, November 2–7, 1981. Ljubljana, Yugoslavia: Research Centre for Co-operation with Developing Countries.

Svetličič, M. *Višenacionalna Preduzeča Zemalja u Razvoju* (Multinational Enterprises of Developing Countries). Ljubljana, Yugoslavia: Research Centre for Co-operation with Developing Countries, 1979.

"Tecnologia Brasileira Operando em Três Continentes." *Comércio y Mercados*, November 1978, p. 20.

Thee, Kian-Wie. "Indonesia as a Host Country to Indian Joint Ventures." In Kumar and McLeod, eds., *Multinationals from Developing Countries*. Lexington, Mass.: Lexington Books, 1981.

Ting, Wen-Lee. "A Comparative Analysis of the Management Technology and Performance of Firms in Newly Industrializing Countries." *Columbia Journal of World Business*, Fall 1980, pp. 83–91.

Ting, Wen-Lee. "New Wave Multinationals Now Compete with Their Western Technology, Marketing Mentors." *Marketing News*, October 17, 1980, section 1, p. 17

Ting, Wen-Lee. "The Product Development Process in NIC Multinationals." Mimeograph, American Graduate School of International Management, Thunderbird Campus, Glendale, Arizona, n.d. (1981?).

Ting, Wen-Lee. "Transfer of Intermediate Technology by Third-World Multinationals." Mimeograph, Tatung Institute of Technology, n.d. (1979?).

Ting, Wen-Lee, and Chi Schive. "Direct Investment and Technology Transfer from Taiwan." In Kumar and McLeod, eds., *Multinationals from Developing Countries*. Lexington, Mass.: Lexington Books, 1981.

Trputec, Zoran. "The Rationale for Developing Countries' Joint Ventures." Presented at International Workshop on the Promotion of Economic and Technical Co-operation among Developing Countries, Bled, Yugoslavia, November 2–7, 1981. Ljubljana, Yugoslavia: Research Centre for Co-operation with Developing Countries.

United Nations Centre on Transnational Corporations. "Measures Taken by Governments to Strengthen their Negotiating Capacity: Joint Ventures between Latin American Enterprises." Report of the Secretariat to the Eighth Session of the Commission on Transnational Corporations, United Nations Economic and Social Council, New York, E/C.10/1982/15, June 25, 1982.

UNCTAD. "Joint Enterprises in Developing Asian, Arab and African Regions." Mimeograph for International Meeting on Latin American Joint Enterprises and Investments, Medellin, Colombia, July 13–15, 1977.

Vernon, Raymond. "Opportunities and Challenges for Multinational Firms from Developing Countries." Seminar Series No. 24, Korea International Economic Institute, Seoul, August 1979.

Weintraub, Peter, and B. H. S. Jayewardene. "Singapore Looks Further Afield." *Far Eastern Economic Review*, May 12, 1978, pp. 40–45.

Wells, Louis T., Jr. "Foreign Investment from the Third World: The Experience of Chinese Firms from Hong Kong." *Columbia Journal of World Business*, Spring 1978.

Wells, Louis T., Jr. "Foreign Investors from the Third World." In Kumar and McLeod, eds., *Multinationals from Developing Countries*. Lexington, Mass.: Lexington Books, 1981.

Wells, Louis T., Jr. "La Internacionalización de Firmas de los Países en Desarrollo." *Integración Latinoamericana*, vol. 2, no. 14, June 1977, pp. 24+.

Wells, Louis T., Jr. "The Internationalization of Firms from the Developing Countries." In Agmon and Kindleberger, eds. *Multinationals from Small Countries*. Cambridge, Mass.: MIT Press, 1977.

Wells, Louis T., Jr. "Multinationals from Asian Developing Countries." Paper presented at Conference on International Transfer of Resources: Strategic Company Responses in the Dynamic Asia Pacific Environment, sponsored by the University of Washington, Montreal, October 17–19, 1981. Mimeograph.

Wells, Louis T., Jr. "Multinationals from Latin American and Asian Developing Countries: How They Differ." *Integración Latinoamericana* (forthcoming).

Wells, Louis T., Jr. "Strategies of Multinational Firms: New Third World Multinationals." *Tatung Life*, January 1, 1980.

Wells, Louis T., Jr. "Technology and Third World Multinationals." The MULTI Working Paper Series, International Labour Office, Geneva, 1982.

Wells, Louis T., Jr. "Third World Multinationals." *Multinational Business*, no. 1, 1980.

Wells, Louis T., Jr., and Pankaj Ghemawat. "Transfer of Industrial Technology among the Developing Countries." Mimeograph, Council on Science and Technology, 1981.

Wells, Louis T., Jr., and V'Ella Warren. "Developing Country Investors in Indonesia." *Bulletin of Indonesian Economic Studies*, March 1979, pp. 69–84.

White, Eduardo. *Empresas Multinacionales Latinoamericanas: la Perspectiva del Derecho Económico*. Mexico City: Fondo de Cultura Económica, 1973.

White, Eduardo. "La Internacionalización de las Empresas Argentinas." *Informe Industrial*, Buenos Aires, January 1979.

White, Eduardo. "The International Projection of Firms from Latin American Countries." In Kumar and McLeod, eds., *Multinationals from Developing Countries*. Lexington, Mass.: Lexington Books, 1981.

White, Eduardo, and Jaime Campos. "Elementos para el Estudio de las Empresas Conjuntas Latinoamericanas." INTAL, Study #17, Buenos Aires, n.d.

White, Eduardo, Jaime Campos, and Guillermo Ondarte. *Las Empresas Conjuntas Latinoamericanas*. Buenos Aires: Instituto para la Integración de America Latina, 1977.

Wu, Yuan-li and Chun-hsi Wu. *Economic Development in Southeast Asia: The Chinese Dimension*. Stanford, Calif.: Hoover Institution, 1980.

Yoshihara, Kunio. *Foreign Investment and Domestic Response: A Study of Singapore's Industrialization*. Singapore: Eastern University Press, 1976.

Index